BestMasters

Springer awards "BestMasters" to the best application-oriented master's theses, which were completed at renowned chairs of economic sciences in Germany, Austria, and Switzerland in 2014.

The works received highest marks and were recommended for publication by supervisors. As a rule, they show a high degree of application orientation and deal with current issues from different fields of economics.

The series addresses practitioners as well as scientists and offers guidance for early stage researchers.

Max Schöne

Real Options Valuation

The Importance of Stochastic Process Choice in Commodity Price Modelling

Springer Gabler

Max Schöne
Vallendar, Germany

Masterthesis,WHU – Otto Beisheim School of Management, 2014

ISBN 978-3-658-07492-0 ISBN 978-3-658-07493-7 (eBook)
DOI 10.1007/978-3-658-07493-7

The Deutsche Nationalbibliothek lists this publication in the Deutsche Nationalbibliografie; detailed bibliographic data are available in the Internet at http://dnb.d-nb.de.

Library of Congress Control Number: 2014952322

Springer Gabler

Printed on acid-free paper

Springer Gabler is a brand of Springer DE.
Springer DE is part of Springer Science+Business Media.
www.springer-gabler.de

Foreword

Commodity prices are an important input factor for capital investment decisions, for instance when it comes to valuation of oil fields, mines or chemical plant configurations to name but a few areas of application. One investment appraisal method which allows to explicitly quantify managerial flexibility is real options valuation which requires the proper specification of the underlying – typically the commodity price – in terms of a stochastic process. Most of the literature relies on the assumption that commodity prices are characterised by Geometric Brownian Motion (GBM) which entails mathematical tractability. Max Schöne, as a starting point for his Master's Thesis, questions this premise and sets out to explore alternative stochastic processes to model commodity price processes providing a better fit to historical data.

Schöne devises in his thesis a calibration scheme which allows him to assess the fit of the investigated processes to a basket of commodities. He finds that the alternatives to GBM provide a better fit and singles out the variance gamma process as the best compromise between goodness of fit and model complexity. He then goes on to demonstrate that the more appropriate specification of the commodity price process for the purpose of real options valuation may affect both project values by as much as 20% and the optimal time to invest.

This thesis therefore serves for the practitioner in capital investment valuation as an excellent source for model selection and for the researcher as a solid starting point for enhanced commodity price modelling.

Prof. Dr. Stefan Spinler

Table of contents

List of figures IX

List of tables XI

List of abbreviations XIII

1 Introduction 1

1.1 Problem and objective 2

1.2 Course of investigation 4

2 Data 6

3 Empirical analysis 9

3.1 Stationarity of prices 9

3.2 Analysis of returns 22

3.2.1 Stylised properties 23

3.2.2 Jumps and GARCH effects 32

4 Modelling commodity prices 40

4.1 Stochastic processes 41

4.1.1 Stochastic volatility 45

4.1.2 Jump diffusion 47

4.1.3 Lévy processes 51

4.2 Model selection 57

4.2.1 Calibration 57

4.2.2 Goodness of fit 62

5 Capital budgeting implications 67

5.1 A stylised investment project 67

5.2 Results 72

6 Conclusion 76

Appendix 79

References 97

List of figures

1 Implications of stationarity 13
2 Variance ratio test 18
3 Backtesting the assumption of mean reversion 20
4 Sample ACF and PACF 25
5 Kernel and normal density 32
6 Time-varying volatility 33
7 Discontinuous price trajectory 37
8 Spectographic jump test 39
9 The Heston model: Parameter sensitivities 48
10 The Merton model: Parameter sensitivities 50
11 The VG model: Parameter sensitivities 53
12 The NIG model: Parameter sensitivities 55
13 The NIG-CIR model: Parameter sensitivities 56
14 Comparing MLE and APDF 61
15 Capital investment project: Valuation analysis 74

List of tables

1 Overview of commodities in the dataset 7
2 Augmented Dickey-Fuller test results 16
3 Moments of commodity returns 28
4 Stationarity, independence, and normality of returns 30
5 Stochastic volatility and normality 34
6 MLE and APDF model fit 62
7 Average squared fitting errors 64
8 Capital investment project: Valuation results 73

List of abbreviations

ACF	Autocorrelation function
AD	Anderson-Darling
ADF	Augmented Dickey-Fuller test
AIC	Akaike information criterion
APDF	Algorithmic probability density fitting
ASE	Average squared error
CIR	Cox-Ingersoll-Ross
DCF	Discounted cash flow
DE	Differential evolution
DoF	Degrees of freedom
EMH	Efficient market hypothesis
GARCH	Generalised Autoregressive Conditional Heteroscedasticity
GBM	Geometric Brownian Motion
IQR	Interquartile range
JB	Jarque-Bera
LB	Ljung-Box
LME	London Metal Exchange
LSM	Least squares Monte Carlo
MLE	Maximum likelihood estimation
MSE	Mean squared error
NIG	Normal inverse Gaussian
NPV	Net present value
OLS	Ordinary least squares
PACF	Partial autocorrelation function
PS	Pattern search
RW	Random walk
SA	Simulated annealing

SDE	Stochastic differential equation
S&P GSCI	Standard & Poors Goldman Sachs commodity index
SSE	Sum of squared errors
VG	Variance Gamma

1 Introduction

The success or failure of businesses is determined by the ability of management to systematically seize value creating investment opportunities. To this end, an accurate investment valuation is of paramount importance as it resembles the only broad and long-term oriented criterion for investment decision making (Brealey, Allen, & Myers, 2011; Koller, Wessels, & Goedhart, 2010).

While Discounted Cash Flow (DCF) and Net Present Value (NPV) analyses are the easiest and most widespread methods to obtain an estimate of project value, they fail to account for the value of managerial flexibility inherent in most investment decisions (Trigeorgis, 1996). Accordingly, Copeland and Antikarov (2003) argue that "NPV systematically undervalues every project" (p. 5), and thereby reinforce the findings of Bhappu and Guzman (1995) and K. Roberts and Weitzman (as cited in Schulmerich, 2010), who contend that even negative NPV projects may be worthwhile to undertake in cases of sequential decision making. Since, very few managerial decisions are completely irreversible or alterable (Copeland & Antikarov, 2003), the idea of Dixit and Pindyck (1994) to capture the arising value of flexibility using options theory, revolutionised the world of corporate finance and laid the foundation for the concept of real option valuation.

Although, this option-based framework unites indisputable benefits in capturing the full ramifications of uncertainty and flexibility in investment valuation, it comes at the cost of higher complexity. In particular, to capture the value arising from management's ability to revise decisions contingent on the future state of the world, it is of central importance to make realistic assumptions on the probability distribution of future events. If this was not the case, one would account for the value of contingent actions based on outcomes that are unrealistic in magnitude or frequency in the first place. Clearly, under such a scenario valuation results cannot be meaningful and reliable.

In real options analysis, the role of simulating future events accrues to a stochastic process that drives the evolution of prices, costs, or output (Copeland & Antikarov, 2003). Moreover, one or more of these quantities are often driven by uncertain future commodity prices as these represent the selling price for natural resource producers such as mining companies (Brennan & Schwartz, 1985), petroleum firms (Siegel, Smith, & Paddock, 1987), or agricultural enterprises (Nissanke, 2012) and in other cases may account for a significant share of production costs at industrial firms. While not only the investment volume in those sectors is high,[1] it has also become increasingly challenging for businesses to cope with the uncertainty of volatile commodity prices in managerial decision making (Schuh, Strohmer, & Zetterqvist, 2011). As a result, the concept of option based valuation is as timely as ever but, at the same time, relies critically on the ability of managers and investors to model the stochastic evolution of future commodity prices appropriately. However, as outlined in more detail in the following subsection "empirical studies on commodity markets are sparse" (Brooks & Prokopczuk, 2013, p. 528) and often provide little practical guidance for the choice of stochastic models in commodity-linked capital investment valuation.

1.1 Problem and objective

The choice of stochastic process matters in real option valuation (Laughton & Jacoby, 1993; Tsekrekos, Shackleton, & Wojakowski, 2012), however, the spectrum of stochastic processes that has been considered in this context is narrow compared to the array of research available on financial options (Brooks & Prokopczuk, 2013). In fact, the majority of studies on option-based capital investment valuation relies on two types of processes (Ozorio, Bastian-Pinto, & Brandao, 2011). First, Geometric Brownian Motion (GBM), as suggested by Black and Scholes (1973) and Cox, Ross, and Rubinstein (1979), is used, among others, by Brennan and Schwartz (1985), Siegel et al. (1987), and Copeland and Antikarov (2003).

[1] According to Esty (2004), project financing in the natural resource industry alone accounted for more than $34 billion in 2001.

Second, variations of mean-reverting models, are applied, for instance, by Gibson and Schwartz (1990), Ross (1997), Schwartz (1997), Schwartz and Smith (2000), Manoliu and Tompaidis (2002), and Casassus and Collin-Dufresne (2005).[2] Despite thorough justification in each case and general acceptance of several of these processes in the literature, there are likewise a number reasons to question their applicability to capital investment valuation. In particular, the assumptions of normally distributed spot price returns has led to criticism of GBM in the context of both, financial options (Brooks & Prokopczuk, 2013; Cont, 2001; Schoutens, 2003) and real options (Lund, 1992; Metcalf & Hassett, 1995) and also the idea of mean reversion in commodity prices appears debatable. While it is consistent with economic intuition[3] and empirical evidence from the term structure of futures prices (Bessembinder, Coughenour, Seguin, & Smoller, 1995; Casassus & Collin-Dufresne, 2005), Dixit and Pindyck (1994) find similar support in historical price series only for long time spans in excess of 40 years. Moreover, Pindyck (1999) fails to reject a unit root[4] in coal and natural gas data over the period from 1875 to 1996 and requires more than 100 years of data to reach the conclusion of mean reversion in crude oil prices. As, however, investment horizons in capital budgeting are often significantly shorter,[5] it is unclear if mean-reverting models resemble a better choice than GBM in the valuation of commodity-linked contingent claims (Pindyck, 1999).

Besides this ambiguity surrounding the two mainly considered types of stochastic models in a capital investment context, no single comprehensive and practical study is available on the subject. While some of the previously mentioned research

[2]Note that in some models (e.g. the two-factor model of Gibson and Schwartz (1990)) mean reversion is induced through a positive correlation between the spot price and a convenience yield process. In other words, when spot prices rise, an increase in the convenience yield will in turn decrease the drift of the spot price process which "will have a mean reversion effect on the spot commodtiy price" (Schwartz & Miltersen, 1998, p. 34). This approach has to be distinguished from processes of the Ornstein-Uhlenbeck type (e.g. the one-factor model of Schwartz (1997)).

[3]When commodity prices are high, supply should increase as higher cost producers begin to enter the market and thereby drive prices back down. Conversely, when commodity prices are low, higher cost producers will be driven out of the market leading to a decrease in supply and rising prices. Over time, prices are expected to revert to long-run total marginal cost Pindyck (1999).

[4]The concept of unit root tests is discussed in section 3.1.

[5]Siegel et al. (1987), for instance, report that the relinquishment of a real world offshore oil property lease is (only) ten years.

has focused on the development of commodity price models to obtain a better fit to market prices of futures contracts,[6] these reports were mainly grounded on generally accepted theoretical arguments on mean reversion and convenience yield dynamics,[7] but did not pursue the econometric verification of mean reversion in past data. Those studies, however, that undertook an empirical investigation did not analyse the merits of alternative price processes that are more consistent with identified scarce empirical support for mean reversion.[8] Furthermore, the range of commodities covered in these analyses is often narrow so that general conclusions on the relative appropriateness of stochastic processes in different markets are difficult to derive, given the heterogeneity of commodity price dynamics documented by Kat and Oomen (2007).

What follows from the previously presented arguments can be summarised in three main objectives for this paper. First, a preferably broad empirical analysis of commodity price dynamics is necessary to shed additional light on the question of return distributions and mean reversion as it will allow me to verify the appropriateness of currently popular GBM and mean-reverting models in capital investment valuation. Second, potential alternative stochastic processes need to be considered that are more consistent with empirical evidence. Third, it must be clarified whether the choice of different stochastic models has a significant impact on valuation results and optimal investment decision rules, so that we can gauge the extent to which model selection deserves careful attention in practice.

1.2 Course of investigation

The remainder of this thesis is organised as follows. Section two presents the dataset. Next, an empirical assessment of mean reversion in commodity prices and an investigation of the normality of return distributions is provided in part three.

[6] See for instance Schwartz (1997), Schwartz and Smith (2000), or Casassus and Collin-Dufresne (2005).

[7] See Brennan (1991) for further reference on the role of convenience yield modelling.

[8] See Dixit and Pindyck (1994) and Pindyck (1999) for a discussion on mean reversion in historical commodity prices.

Once we have a better understanding of empirical price dynamics, it is investigated what characteristics a stochastic process should possess in order to realistically reproduce empirical price dynamics. Accordingly, a range of potential models with different properties is outlined in the first half of section four. Subsequently, a practical and flexible calibration method is proposed that facilitates the assessment of relative goodness of fit of each process to different commodity data. Based on the calibrated price models it is analysed in section five to what extent process choice influences the valuation of a stylised capital investment project with multiple inherent options. Section six concludes.

2 Data

The task of setting up an appropriate dataset for my purposes involves decisions on the commodities to include, whether to use short-term future contracts or spot price data, what time period to analyse, and what data frequency to use.

Following Marshall, Nguyen, and Visaltanachoti (2012), I focus on the components of the S&P Goldman Sachs Commodity Index (S&P GSCI). As this index comprises 24 *important* commodities spanning energy, industrial metal, precious metal, agriculture, and livestock, it suits my desire to obtain conclusions of preferably broad, cross-sectoral applicability and to account for the heterogeneity of different commodities (Kat & Oomen, 2007).

With respect to the type of price quote to use, I would generally prefer to use spot instead of future prices for my purposes, however, Fama and French (1987) suggest that "good spot-price data are not available for most commodities" (p. 57) and Schwartz (1997) raises similar concerns about their liquidity. As a result, these authors propose the use of short-term futures data instead. Since this view is not shared by Brooks and Prokopczuk (2013) and would generally complicate the analysis and interpretation of results throughout the paper, I conjecture that in the wake of "tremendous growth in commodity [...] markets" (Tsekrekos et al., 2012, p. 543), these earlier findings are not necessarily reflective of spot price data quality in the more recent past.[9] Since the use of justifiable data can be pivotal for the results of any empirical study (Gujarati, 2003), I feel it is necessary to assess the relative data quality in spot and futures markets based on a short, back-of-the-envelope liquidity calculation.

For this task, the simple but computationally feasible[10] *Zeros* measure turns out useful (Lesmond, Ogden, & Trzcinka, 1999). For a given underlying, this met-

[9]Fama and French (1987) and Schwartz (1997) use datasets for the periods 1966 - 1984 and 1985 - 1995, respectively.

[10]Marshall et al. (2012) advise the Amihud (2002) or Effective Tick measure developed by (Goyenko, Holden, & Trzcinka, 2009) to calculate the liquidity of a security, however, these measures rely on trading volume data or price spreads, which are not consistently available from Thomson Reuters for spot price data of S&P GSCI components.

Table 1:

Overview of commodities in the dataset

BBL: Barrel, BSH: Bushel, FED: U.S. Federal Reserve, ICCO: International Cocoa Organization, ISO: International Sugar Organization, LBM: London Bullion Market, LME: London Metal Exchange, MT: Metric Ton, OZT: Troy Ounce, TR: Thomson Reuters, USDA: U.S. Department of Agriculture. Note that the data is presented following the logic of four distinctive areas: Energy, industrial metals, precious metals, and agriculture. The sample period for all items is from 02/08/1993 to 30/12/2013. All data are in US$.

Name	Code	Full description	Unit	Source
Crude oil	CRUDOIL	Crude Oil-WTI Spot Cushing	BBL	TR
Aluminum	LAHCASH	LME-Aluminium 99.7% Cash	MT	LME
Copper	LCPCASH	LME-Copper Grade A Cash	"	"
Lead	LEDCASH	LME-Lead Cash	"	"
Nickel	LNICASH	LME-Nickel Cash	"	"
Zinc	LZZCASH	LME-SHG Zinc 99.995% Cash	"	"
Gold	GOLDBLN	Gold Bullion LBM	OZT	LBM
Silver	SLVCASH	Silver Fix LBM Cash	"	"
Wheat	WHEATHD	Wheat, No.2 Hard (Kansas)	BSH	USDA
Corn	COTSCIL	Corn US No.2 South Central IL	"	"
Soybeans	SOYADSC	Yellow Soybn US NO.1 Sth Dvprt	"	"
Sugar	WSUGDLY	Raw Sugar-ISA	LB	ISO
Coffee	COFBRAZ	Coffee-Brazilian (NY)	"	TR
Cocoa	COCINUS	Cocoa-ICCO	MT	ICCO

ric relies on the proven negative relationship between the number of trading days with zero returns and liquidity in a given time interval. Hence, we can gain a rudimentary understanding of the relative liquidity and data quality of spot and future prices by simply comparing the average number of zero-return trading days per interval in both markets. As directly comparable spot and 3-months future prices are only available from the London Metal Exchange (LME) for the industrial metals part of the S&P GSCI index, this short liquidity analysis is somewhat limited in scope, but, nonetheless, the exercise reveals that over the more recent past LME data quality is, in fact, higher for spot prices than future prices. By investigating the development of *Zeros* over time, this conclusion can be reconciled with previous research as it shows unsatisfactory spot price data quality prior to July 1993, but a structural improvement thereafter. To conserve space, the graphical results of this analysis are provided in appendix A1.

Following the previous argument, I use spot price data for all commodities with

satisfactory data availability for the period 02/08/1993 - 30/12/2013. With respect to the data frequency, I use weekly quotes in the majority of calculations, as I suspect these to be more reflective of decision making horizons in capital investment decisions. However, as the analysis of empirical time series properties and calibration tasks can sometimes benefit from the information contained in more frequent daily returns, I follow Kat and Oomen (2007) and Brooks and Prokopczuk (2013) and resort to daily quotes in some cases.
An overview of the 14 commodities in the dataset is given in table 1. A complementary graph showing the historical price evolution for the four commodity sectors and the S&P 500 equity index is given in appendix A2. A table with all non-trading dates that have been erased from the dataset for the previous and all subsequent analyses is given in appendix A3. Please note that it is due to limited availability of high quality spot price data for energy commodities and live stock that only 14 out of the 24 S&P GSCI components are used.

3 Empirical analysis

As a first step to a better understanding of commodity price dynamics, it is useful to exploit the rich set of information contained in historical price series via a range of econometric and statistical tests. Although, one may be sceptical that a backward looking analysis can yield valuable insights for the decision of how to model seemingly random price movements in the future, more than half a century of empirical studies have revealed that the statistical properties of such price variations are indeed common across numerous asset classes in different markets and time periods (Cont, 2001; Mantegna & Stanley, 2000). For my purposes, it is logical to split the empirical analysis into two main blocks. First, it is analysed whether commodity prices are mean-reverting. The answer to this question is a corner stone in this thesis, as it resembles a central assumption to distinguish between stochastic processes. Second, we will assess whether commodity returns are normally distributed.

3.1 Stationarity of prices

Following from the previous discussion, the question of mean-reverting prices is the principal distinctive assumption between commonly used GBM and mean-reverting processes. Broadly speaking, a stochastic process is mean-reverting (interchangeably we may refer to such a process as stationary or one without unit root) if its mean and variance are constant over time and the covariance between two observations depends only on the lag between them but not on the time when it is computed (Gujarati, 2003).[11] On the contrary, a non-stationary price process is characterised by a growing and unlimited variance over time that allows prices to rise without bound. To see more explicitly how the property of mean reversion

[11]In the literature, this form of stationarity is known as weak stationarity. In the case of a strictly stationary series all moments of the probability distribution are invariant over time (Cryer & Chan, 2008).

enters a stochastic process let us consider

$$S_t = \theta S_{t-1} + \varepsilon_t, \tag{3.1.1}$$

where S_t denotes, for instance, the price of a commodity at time t, θ the autoregressive coefficient, and ε_t a white noise process[12]. In this framework, the absolute value of θ is governing the mechanics of mean reversion. In particular, we distinguish between two cases. First, the non-stationary Random Walk (RW) process, where $|\theta| = 1$ and, second, the stationary AR(1) process where $|\theta| < 1$.[13] As a deeper understanding of the link between θ, process variance, and stationarity is very beneficial for subsequent statistical testing, let us study these cases in greater detail. To begin with, it is useful to apply repeated backward substitution to rewrite our expression for S_t as

$$S_t = \theta\left[\theta\left[\theta S_{t-3} + \varepsilon_{t-2}\right] + \varepsilon_{t-1}\right] + \varepsilon_t = \theta^3 S_{t-3} + \theta^2 \varepsilon_{t-2} + \theta \varepsilon_{t-1} + \varepsilon_t. \tag{3.1.2}$$

Considering now the case where $\theta = 1$, it can be seen that if we continue to substitute S and set the initial price to zero, the above equation simplifies to

$$S_t = \sum_{i=0}^{t} \varepsilon_i. \tag{3.1.3}$$

This illustrates that under a RW model, the price of e.g. a commodity at an arbitrary point in time t is given by a sequence of random shocks, where the impact of every individual shock never fades away over time. Intuitively, this also explains why the range of possible outcomes and, hence, the variance of this non-stationary process should grow over time. To see more formally why this is the case let use consider the Mean Squared Error (MSE) of a price forecast in a RW process s periods ahead.

[12]White noise refers to a series of serially uncorrelated innovations with a mean of zero and a constant non-negative variance (Gujarati, 2003).

[13]Note that when $\theta = 0$, (3.1.1) collapses to a (stationary) white noise process.

Hence, we are interested in the quantity

$$MSE_s = E\left[\left(S_{t+s} - \hat{S}_{t+s}\right)^2\right], \tag{3.1.4}$$

where $E[S_{t+s}]$ is the conditional expectation of S_t s periods ahead and $E\left[\hat{S}_{t+s}\right]$ the unconditional expectation. Since S_t can be expressed according to (3.1.3), we can write for the case with an initial price different from zero

$$MSE_s = E\left[(S_t + \sum_{i=1}^{s} \varepsilon_{t+i} - \hat{S}_{t+s})^2\right].$$

However, since the best unconditional estimate for the future price in this Markovian setting $\hat{S}_{t+s}$ is simply today's price S_t and $var(\varepsilon_t) = \sigma^2$, we get

$$MSE_s = E\left[\left(\sum_{i=1}^{s} \varepsilon_{t+i}\right)^2\right] = s\sigma^2. \tag{3.1.5}$$

Hence, the variance of this non-stationary process grows linearly in time (s) and the volatility at the square root of time.
In the second case where $|\theta| < 1$, we can observe in (3.1.2) that the influence of the past on current prices is declining in time, thereby restraining the process to fluctuate around its unconditional mean (zero in our example). To quantify this dynamic we are, again, interested in an analytic expression for the variance as a function of time. To compute MSE_s recap that $cov(\varepsilon_t, \varepsilon_{t+s}) = 0$ (for $s \neq 0$) and that the unconditional expectation of an AR(1) process is given by $E[S_{t+s} \mid S_t, \ldots, S_0] = \theta^s S_t$. As a first step, let us consider

$$\begin{aligned} MSE_3 = E\left[\left(S_{t+3} - \hat{S}_{t+3}\right)^2\right] &= E\left[\left(\theta^3 S_t + \theta^2 \varepsilon_{t+1} + \theta\varepsilon_{t+2} + \varepsilon_{t+3} - \theta^3 S_t\right)^2\right] \\ &= \sigma^2\left(1 + \theta^2 + \theta^4\right), \end{aligned}$$

where the conditional expectation S_{t+3} is obtained by adapting the time index of (3.1.2). Computing MSE also at some other values of s, one will soon recognise the pattern that leads to the following generalisation for s periods:

$$MSE_s = \sigma^2 \left(1+\theta^2+\cdots+\theta^{2s-2}\right).$$

Applying now a simple mathematical trick, we multiply the previous expression by θ^2 to get

$$\theta^2 MSE_s = \sigma^2 \left(\theta^2+\cdots+\theta^{2s}\right)$$

and subtract the result again from the previous equation. Simplifying yields

$$MSE_s \left(1-\theta^2\right) = \sigma^2 \left(1+\theta^{2s}\right)$$

$$MSE_s = \sigma^2 \frac{\left(1+\theta^{2s}\right)}{1-\theta^2}. \tag{3.1.6}$$

To see that this conditional variance converges to the unconditional variance as an upper bound as s increases, we can take the limit of (3.1.6) and obtain

$$\lim_{s\to\infty} = V[S_t] = \frac{\sigma^2}{1-\theta^2}. \tag{3.1.7}$$

While it took us some steps to work through this exercise, it will soon become apparent how the role of process variance and the coefficient θ are intimately related to subsequent stationarity tests and the underlying principles of common stochastic processes. In fact, all stochastic diffusion models are closely related to (3.1.1). GBM, for instance, is roughly speaking a RW with drift in continuous time that restricts prices to remain positive over time (Björk, 2009). On the other hand, Ornstein-Uhlenbeck processes such as the popular Vasicek (1977) model are, in some variation, the continuous time limit of the simple AR(1) process. To round off the introductory discussion of stationarity, please consider fig. 1 for a graphical illustration of the impact θ has on simulated price trajectories. Turning now to the actual question of this subsection, namely whether historical commodity prices are mean-reverting, we will first directly test the value of θ and, second, analyse the

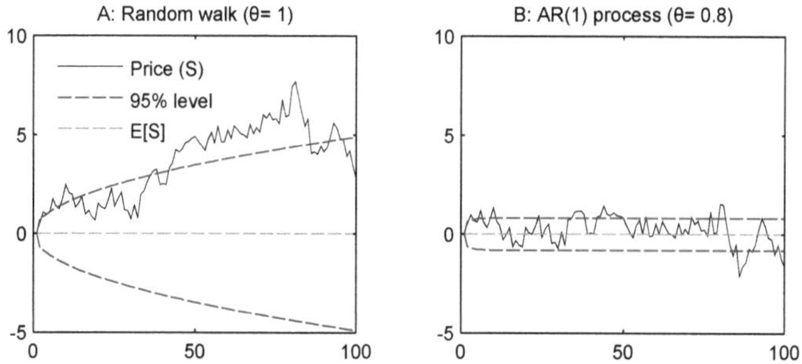

Figure 1: Implications of stationarity. Panel A illustrates the non-stationary behaviour of a random walk without drift and standard deviation $\sigma = 0.15$. Panel B shows a stationary AR(1) process with unconditional long-term mean of zero and an autoregressive coefficient $\theta = 0.8$ as shown above. Both processes are computed with the identical pseudo random numbers over 100 simulation steps.

development of empirical price variance over time to make inferences on stationarity.

A common test of the hypothesis $H_0 : |\theta| = 1$ against the alternative $H_1 : |\theta| < 1$ is the Augmented Dickey-Fuller (ADF) test developed by Dickey and Fuller (1979, 1981). The test involves a regression of the following kind:

$$S_t = \alpha + \delta t + \theta S_{t-1} + \beta_1 \Delta S_{t-1} + \beta_2 \Delta S_{t-2} + \cdots + \beta_p \Delta S_{t-p} + \varepsilon_t, \qquad (3.1.8)$$

where S_t denotes the natural logarithm of the commodity price.[14] $\beta \Delta S$ are added to control for serial correlation among the innovations (ε) and $\Delta S = S_t - S_{t-1}$. The lag order is given by p and α and δt denote a drift and deterministic time trend, respectively. While drift and trend can be excluded, they allow to test the unit root hypothesis more accurately for different data characteristics. In other words, if the data series shows a linear trend, the term δt can be added to control for the trend and test the hypothesis of trend stationarity. If the data instead exhibits no linear trend but seems to have a non-zero mean, the drift term α should be added.[15]

To account for the possibility of these data characteristics, I run the regression

[14]Taking logs is often advised in the literature if a series shows exponential growth to establish a better fit in linear regressions. See, for instance, Pindyck (1999).

[15]For a comprehensive overview on the ADF test see Gujarati (2003), Cryer and Chan (2008), or Franke, Härdle, and Hafner (2011).

(3.1.8) in three different specifications. First, as an autoregressive model without drift and deterministic time trend (AR), second, as an autoregressive model with drift (ARD), and, third, as a trend stationarity model with drift and deterministic time trend (TS).

For each of these model specifications, the optimal lag order is determined as follows. First, the maximum number of lags is computed according to (3.1.9) as proposed by Schwert (1989). Subsequently, the ADF test is programmatically run for all lags $p = p_{max}, \ldots, 1$ and the Akaike Information Criterion (AIC)[16] of the regression is recorded at each step. Following Gujarati (2003), I set the lag order corresponding to the lowest AIC, i.e. the one that yields the best model fit.

$$p_{max} = \left\lfloor 12 \left(\frac{T}{100} \right)^{\frac{1}{4}} \right\rfloor \tag{3.1.9}$$

What follows from the consideration to allow for a higher lag order, is the question of the appropriate test statistic. In line with common practice, I use

$$t^1_{\hat{\theta}} = \frac{\hat{\theta} - 1}{\text{se}} \tag{3.1.10}$$

where $\hat{\theta}$ is the Ordinary Least Squares (OLS) estimate of θ and *se* its standard error. However, to be conservative, a lag-adjusted, unstudentised t-statistic given in (3.1.11) is additionally used for comparison. Here, N is the effective sample size, adjusted for lags.

$$t^2_{\hat{\theta}} = \frac{N(\hat{\theta} - 1)}{(1 - \beta_1 - \cdots - \beta_p)} \tag{3.1.11}$$

Keeping in mind the heterogeneity of commodity price evolution in different time periods (see appendix A2) and the consideration of Pindyck (1999) and Gujarati (2003) that test results may strongly differ depending on the sample period under consideration, the ADF test is run on several sub-samples of the dataset and both

[16] See Akaike (1973) for further reference.

weekly and daily price quotes. A representative snapshot of these results is given in table 2. Before turning to an interpretation, let us briefly consider the choice of the two different sample periods analysed. First, the full sample period (1993-2013) is considered based on the motivation to get a preferably broad picture of price dynamics over a long time horizon. The choice of the second period from 1993 to 2004 is motivated by the desire to exclude time periods that are, arguably, abnormal in some sense and not representative for price dynamics in general. For instance, given the strong link of commodity markets to global finance (Nissanke, 2012), the financial crisis, beginning in 2007[17], has presumably contributed to *un-natural* price dynamics thereafter. However, M. Roberts and Schlenker (2013) point out that a seemingly unusual ascent of commodity prices began even earlier in 2005, so that is appears conservative in an assessment of mean reversion to run the test on a period ending well ahead of these events in 2004.

The test results suggest that a unit root can be rejected only for silver and corn and even in these cases, the result is not persistent across different time periods. While the analysis of other time periods and test statistics does not change the direction of these results, it must be noted that beyond the findings reported here, over the period from 1993 to 2006, one can reject a unit root for soybeans in a model with drift and on the basis of daily data for crude oil in the trend stationary model over the full sample period. While these findings imply little empirical support of mean-reverting models, Dixit and Pindyck (1994) and Pindyck (1999) would advise us to be cautious in the interpretation. They argue that for short time series, the ADF test often fails to reject a unit root in actually mean-reverting data. Additionally, it has to be taken into account that the failure to reject a unit root does not imply its acceptance.

Hence, some further clarification is necessary before any conclusions can be drawn. More specifically, it is useful to analyse also the extent to which price shocks are temporary or permanent (Pindyck, 1999). The logic of this test follows from the

[17]On 9 August 2007, BNP Paribas announced that it was ceasing activity in three hedge funds specialised in U.S. mortgage debt as they were no longer able to assess their value and risk (Elliot, 2011).

Table 2:

Augmented Dickey-Fuller test results

AR: Model without drift and deterministic trend, ARD: Model with drift only, TS: Model with drift and deterministic time trend. The test statistic t refers to $t^1_{\hat{\theta}}$, given by (3.1.10) and *,**,*** indicate that a unit root can be rejected at the 10%, 5%, and 1% confidence level, respectively. The corresponding p-value is denoted by p and indicates the error probability if a unit root is rejected. Sample periods start on 02/08/1993 and end on 30/12/2013 and 27/12/2004 depending on the sample. Data frequency is weekly.

		AR		ARD		TS	
Resource	Sample	t	p	t	p	t	p
Oil	1993 - 2013	1.01	0.92	-1.01	0.73	-2.89	0.17
	1993 - 2004	0.48	0.82	-1.67	0.44	-2.91	0.16
Aluminum	1993 - 2013	0.39	0.79	-2.20	0.21	-2.29	0.45
	1993 - 2004	0.75	0.88	-2.14	0.23	-2.15	0.52
Copper	1993 - 2013	1.11	0.93	-0.66	0.85	-1.60	0.79
	1993 - 2004	0.63	0.85	-0.91	0.78	-0.65	0.98
Lead	1993 - 2013	1.18	0.94	-1.15	0.68	-1.95	0.62
	1993 - 2004	1.10	0.93	-1.30	0.61	-1.30	0.89
Nickel	1993 - 2013	0.63	0.85	-1.69	0.43	-1.90	0.64
	1993 - 2004	0.97	0.91	-1.24	0.63	-1.68	0.75
Zinc	1993 - 2013	0.62	0.85	-1.44	0.55	-1.98	0.60
	1993 - 2004	0.38	0.79	-2.09	0.26	-2.10	0.54
Gold	1993 - 2013	1.38	0.96	-0.01	0.96	-2.03	0.58
	1993 - 2004	0.18	0.72	-1.19	0.66	-0.81	0.96
Silver	1993 - 2013	0.68	0.86	-0.86	0.80	-2.24	0.48
	1993 - 2004	0.06	0.68	-2.79*	0.06	-2.83	0.19
Wheat	1993 - 2013	-0.67	0.40	-2.10	0.25	-2.51	0.34
	1993 - 2004	-0.86	0.34	-2.11	0.25	-2.16	0.51
Corn	1993 - 2013	-1.91*	0.05	-1.90	0.34	-2.41	0.39
	1993 - 2004	-1.59	0.11	-2.24	0.19	-2.64	0.27
Soybeans	1993 - 2013	0.10	0.69	-1.33	0.59	-2.44	0.37
	1993 - 2004	-0.70	0.39	-2.10	0.25	-2.11	0.54
Sugar	1993 - 2013	0.04	0.67	-1.69	0.43	-2.09	0.55
	1993 - 2004	-0.39	0.51	-1.98	0.30	-2.78	0.21
Coffee	1993 - 2013	0.17	0.71	-2.03	0.29	-1.97	0.60
	1993 - 2004	0.13	0.70	-1.57	0.49	-2.37	0.41
Cocoa	1993 - 2013	0.75	0.88	-1.78	0.40	-2.54	0.32
	1993 - 2004	0.44	0.81	-2.05	0.27	-2.04	0.57

earlier consideration of the difference in the persistence of shocks in the RW and AR(1) process. This time, we are not directly interested in the value of θ, but instead analyse the historical price variance to make inferences on mean reversion. An appropriate tool for this task are variance ratio tests of the sort proposed by Cochrane (1988). The test ratio can be defined as "the sample variance of the k-period differences divided by k times the sample variance of the first difference" (Cecchetti & Pok-sang, 1994, p. 177) and can be calculated according to (3.1.12).

$$vr_k = \frac{1}{k}\frac{var(S_{t+k} - S_t)}{var(S_{t+1} - S_t)} \tag{3.1.12}$$

As in the ADF test, S denotes the natural logarithm of the commodity price. If a series is non-stationary, the numerator of this ratio should grow linearly in k and, hence, vr_k should approach one. Conversely, if the data is stationary the k-period variance should approach an upper limit so that vr_k converges to zero as k grows. Lastly, a ratio rising above one indicates mean aversion, suggesting neither consistency with GBM nor mean-reverting processes (Pindyck, 1999). The variance ratio test results are reported for the previously considered two sample periods and for all commodities to obtain a well justified conclusion (fig. 2).

The findings lead to a similar conclusion as the ADF test. Except for oil and silver none of the commodities display variance ratios that seem to tend towards zero. Finding consistently supporting evidence for mean reversion is even more difficult when considering both sampling periods together.[18]

In summary, it follows from the previous investigation that only silver exhibits mean reversion in both tests. Additionally, there is some evidence for mean reversion in corn, oil, and soybeans, however, these results are not persistent across tests, sample period, or data frequency. While these findings may be explained by a very low speed of mean reversion that can simply not be detected over two decades as suggested by Dixit and Pindyck (1994), it raises nonetheless questions about the appropriateness of mean-reverting price models in real option applica-

[18]Note that additional calculations reveal no sensitivity of the results to the choice of lag order.

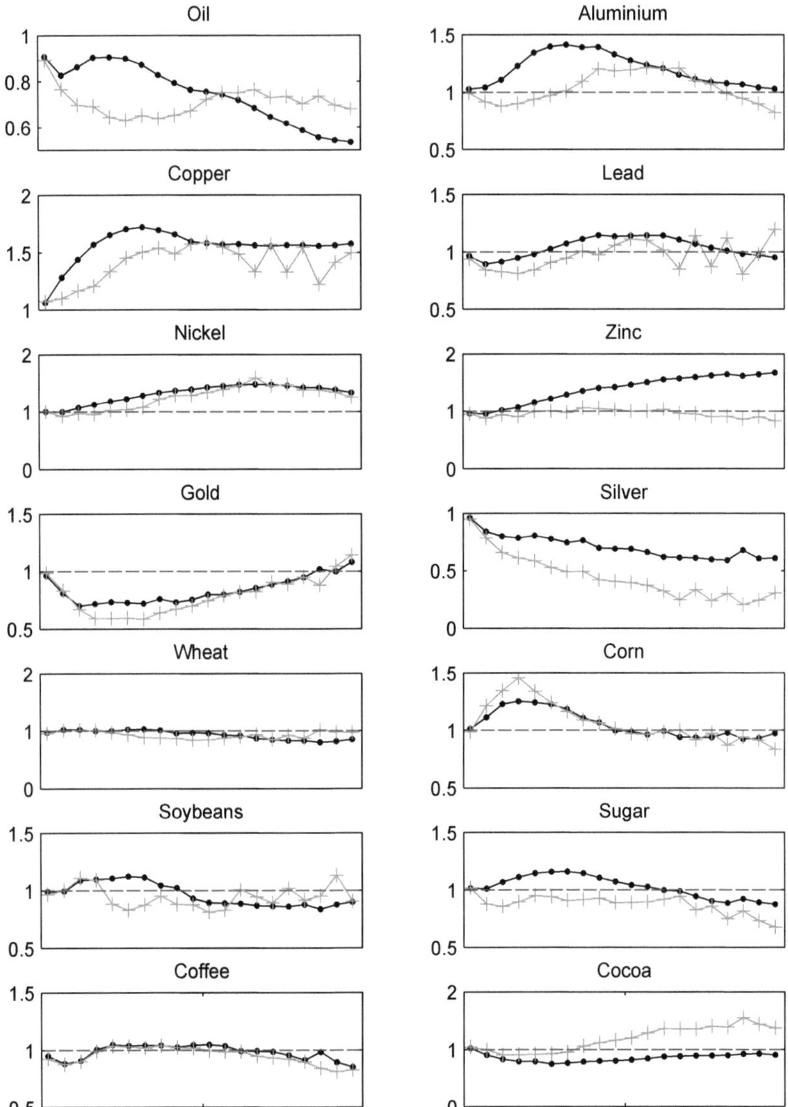

Figure 2: Variance ratio test. This figure shows the variance ratio (y-axis) for 2...100 lags (x-axis). The ratio is calculated over two time periods. First, from 02/08/1993 to 30/12/2013 (black). Second, from 02/08/1993 to 27/12/2004. Also shown is a red reference line for a value consistent with a RW process.

tions. Although, it is difficult to obtain reliable estimates of typical investment horizons in a capital budgeting context, it seems far fetched that these are regularly in excess of 100 years so that mean reversion would play a role in price modelling according to the findings of Dixit and Pindyck (1994) and Pindyck (1999). Instead, the only powerful arguments in favour of applying mean-reverting models are on the theoretical side. Several studies, including those of Laughton and Jacoby (1993), Dixit and Pindyck (1994), Schwartz and Smith (2000), and Sick and Gamba (2010), propagate the use of such models mainly based on the idea that in an equilibrium setting, non-differentiated products, such as commodities, should trade at prices close to their marginal cost of production over the long-run. Indeed, the use of a mathematical model without theoretical support for its assumptions is not a convincing practice, however, I argue that it is just as little convincing to rely on a theory without thorough empirical support. In this regard, it is unclear at this stage what conclusions we should derive from the previous statistical results for our later task to propose meaningful stochastic commodity price models. In fact, before moving on, we should clarify whether the previously identified evidence against mean reversion can also be reconciled with economic intuition so that we can confidently omit the study of mean-reverting models in the remainder of this paper and focus on non-stationary ones instead.

To shed some more light on the question if the assumption of stationary prices is sensible in a real option setting, let us first conduct a brief hands-on experiment to backtest the relative appropriateness of mean reversion on an intuitive level over the past two decades using the previously mentioned stationary Vasicek or Ornstein-Uhlenbeck model and GBM (see fig. 3). Since the technicalities of both models are not yet relevant at this stage, a detailed consideration of GBM is postponed until section 4.1. and some details on the Vasicek process (as far as relevant for this exercise) are presented in appendix B.

Since aluminium price data is available as of 1980, this market is a convenient venue for this task. To be realistic, both processes are calibrated with 15 years

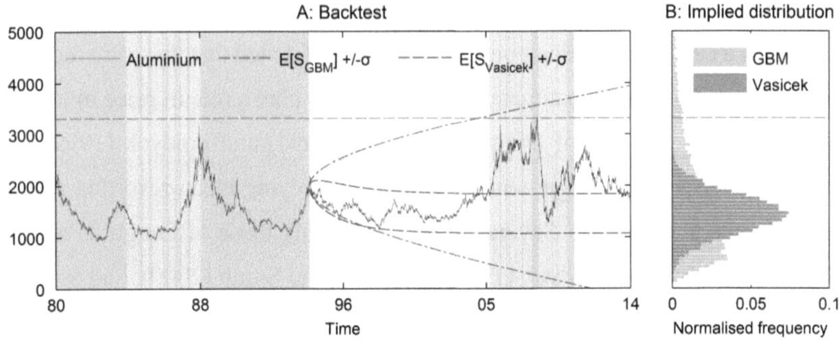

Figure 3: Backtesting the assumption of mean reversion. Panel A shows the historical price evolution of the LME aluminium price. The two shaded time periods from left to right are the model calibration period (02/01/1980 - 30/12/1994) and a period of high volatility (05/09/2005 to 30/08/2010), respectively. Also shown are volatility bounds of GBM and the Vasicek model, which represent the expected value +/- one standard deviation (σ) . Panel B illustrates the price distribution under both processes for the date 11/07/2008, where an intermediate price peak of US$ 3,317 occurred. The distribution is extracted from 10,000 price simulations.

of daily data (1980-1995)[19] and are subsequently compared to realised aluminium prices from 1995 until the end of 2013. Despite even higher volatility in the calibration period than thereafter,[20] it is evident that the implied distribution of prices under the mean-reverting Vasicek process vastly underestimates fluctuations in the real world. In fact, when considering the price peak on 11/07/2008 and the corresponding model price distributions, it stands out that observations of this kind (or above) have zero probability in the Vasicek model but 13 per cent under GBM.

If we imagine now a hypothetical firm assessing the value of a natural hedge against high aluminium prices such as a production facility that allows to switch to a different, less costly input resource in times of high aluminium prices, it becomes clear that the inherent option to switch[21] would have been undervalued on the basis of assuming mean reversion in prices. In other words, if a stochastic process does not assign any probability to contingencies such as the price peak on 11/07/2008,

[19]Both models are calibrated using Maximum Likelihood Estimation (MLE). In the case of GBM this involves estimating the drift and volatility parameter, in the Vasicek model the long-term mean, volatility, and mean-reversion speed. Please see appendix B2 for details.

[20]The annualised volatility of daily log-returns was 21.6 % in the calibration period and 19.9 % in the testing period.

[21]See Tsekrekos et al. (2012) for further reference.

the value of flexibility, i.e. the possibility of contingent action following this event, is not accounted for in the real option analysis. As a result, I argue that even if commodity prices mean revert in the very long-run, it is the distribution of prices implied in mean-reverting stochastic processes that may lead to inaccurate decision making in capital budgeting throughout time.

Moreover, while mean reversion may have been plausible over the past 100 years (Pindyck, 1999), it appears to be a less coherent assumption in more recent times and, presumably, the future. This conjecture relies on two arguments. First, structural supply and demand imbalances have originated from an upsurge in commodity demand from Asia and newly industrialising emerging economies as well as supply constraints that are expected to persist over the medium to long-term (Nissanke, 2012; M. Roberts & Schlenker, 2013). Given the resulting precarious state of demand and supply uncertainty, commodity prices are expected to remain highly dependent on shifts in market expectations and the uncertain growth prospects of the world economy. As a result, it is difficult to picture a realistic long-run mean price level in conjunction with a restricted variance of future outcomes. This argument is supported by Tang (2012), who contends that if commodity prices are modelled as mean-reverting, the mean level needs to be stochastic. Second, commodity markets have witnessed a dramatic increase in derivatives trading and inflow of speculative funds since 1980, which strengthen the link of commodity prices to other asset classes and exacerbate the magnitude of price fluctuations (Erb & Harvey, 2005; Gorton & Rouwenhorst, 2006; Nissanke, 2012). What follows is that commodity prices are repeatedly driven away from presumed equilibrium levels over extended time periods so that any meaningful assumption on mean reversion is difficult to hold.

Conclusively, this section has revealed that there is little empirical support for the assumption of mean reversion in commodity prices over the past two decades. Furthermore, I argue that this may not be counter intuitive or at odds with economic intuition in the wake of structural changes in the global real economy and continuously evolving financial markets.

3.2 Analysis of returns

Given the previous conclusion that the assumption of stationary prices is often difficult to justify in today's commodity markets, we will shift our focus to the analysis of empirical price properties relevant for non-stationary price models. The goal of this section is to gain an understanding if a simple non-stationary model such as GBM is capable of reproducing the (most relevant) statistical properties of past prices in future simulations. If this is not the case, it needs to be understood where deviations between standard model assumptions and reality occur so that solutions can be proposed in later sections.

Please note that all subsequent analyses focus on the behaviour of returns instead of price levels. This is convenient, because the study of any time series with the goal to generalise the identified properties to other time periods or the parametrisation of simulation models requires stationarity of data (Gujarati, 2003). While we have already seen that prices mostly do not fulfil this requirement, Cont (2001) suggests that the distributional properties of returns are more persistent over time. Clearly, prices and returns are just the flipside of the same quantity, however, the study of returns allows us to extract valuable information from the past more readily (Mantegna & Stanley, 2000).

The remainder of this subsection is organised as follows. In the first part, some of the empirical properties of commodity returns are investigated. This involves preliminary tests on return stationarity and independence, as well as tests on the normality of return distributions. The second part is aimed at making a link between the identified statistical properties of returns and stochastic price models. In other words, we will try to identify more explicitly how the empirical findings can be captured by stochastic processes.

3.2.1 Stylised properties

While the list of stylised return properties one can test is long (Cont, 2001; Cont & Tankov, 2004), we will limit our focus to an investigation of those properties that are directly relevant for our purpose of stochastic price modelling in the next section. To begin with, let us define r_t as the log return at time t given by $r_t = \ln(P_t/P_{t-1})$. Please note that log returns are used due to their convenient multiplicative properties and common use in financial theory (Hull, 2009).

As a first step, we will verify whether returns are indeed stationary so that the distributional properties of r remain similar over time. To see why this is necessary, imagine we want to calibrate a stochastic process to past return data and use the resulting parameters for future price simulations as we did in fig. 3. Clearly, for the results to be meaningful, the distribution of r must remain largely unchanged during the calibration and analysis period. Now, to test stationarity we will resort to the ADF test and run it on past weekly returns. As this test has already been discussed before, we jump directly to the results shown in table 4. In line with expectations, a unit root can be rejected for all commodities at the one per cent confidence level so that the above postulated requirement is satisfied.

Next, it is analysed if returns are independent. This is a common assumption in many (non-stationary) stochastic processes and it is intimately linked to economic theory. In other words, if markets are efficient, we would expect current prices to reflect all available and predictable information. What remains to drive prices must be unpredictable new information that is by definition random (Fama, 1965; Samuelson, 1964). If this is so, we would expect the absence of any systematic link between today's and tomorrow's prices, i.e. we would expect returns to be independent random shocks. To verify this conjecture, we check for autocorrelation in historical returns (Brigo, Dalessandro, Neugebauer, & Triki, 2007). For this purpose, the Ljung-Box (LB) test proposed by Ljung and Box (1978), and the Autocorrelation Function (ACF) and Partial Autocorrelation Function (PACF) advocated by Brigo et al. (2007) are used.

The *LB* test compares the null hypothesis that our series of returns exhibits no autocorrelation for a certain number of lags L with the alternative that some autocorrelation coefficient $\rho(t)$, $t = 1, \ldots, L$ is different from zero. The test statistic is computed according to

$$LB = T(T+2)\sum_{t=1}^{L}\left(\frac{\rho(t)^2}{(T-t)}\right), \tag{3.2.1}$$

where T is the sample size, L the number of lags at which the autocorrelation ρ is evaluated. The test static follows a chi-square distribution with L degrees of freedom (Gujarati, 2003). In line with Kat and Oomen (2007), ten lags are used in the test. The results are shown in table 4, indicating that in the case of crude oil, copper, nickel, gold, and coffee, the null hypothesis of independent returns must be rejected. As this statistical relation between observations at different lags is unexpected and inconsistent with many stochastic processes, a graphical analysis of the *ACF* and *PACF* is provided to judge the severity of this finding. The *ACF* at lag t is given by

$$ACF_k = \frac{1}{T}\sum_{t=1}^{T-k}(r_t - \hat{\mu})(r_{t+k} - \hat{\mu}), \qquad k = 0, 1, 2, \ldots, K \tag{3.2.2}$$

where k denotes the lag at which the function is evaluated, K the maximum number of lags up to which the analysis is carried out, T the number of observations, and $\hat{\mu}$ the sample mean. Before turning to an interpretation of results, let me also introduce the *PACF* as it is often considered complementary to the *ACF* (Brigo et al., 2007). While the ACF_k yields an estimate of the correlation between $r(t)$ and $r(t+k)$, $PACF_k$ indicates the correlation between these observations that is not explained by intermediate lags $1, \ldots, k-1$ (Gujarati, 2003). According to Brigo et al. (2007), the *PACF* is roughly a sample estimate of the quantity

$$cor\left(r_t - \bar{r}^{t}_{t+1,\ldots,t+k-1}, r_{t+k} - \bar{r}^{t+k}_{t+1,\ldots,t+k-1}\right), \tag{3.2.3}$$

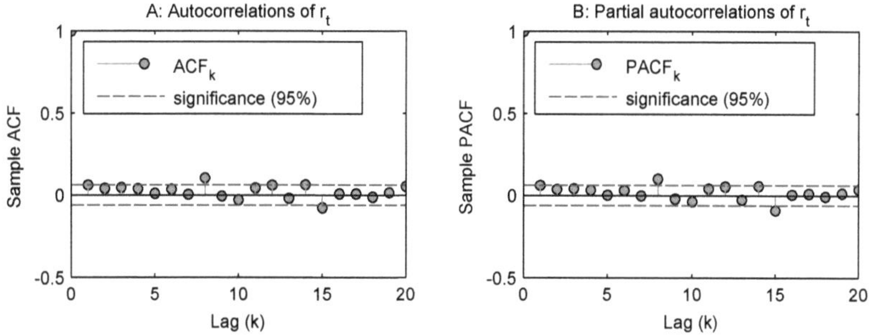

Figure 4: Sample ACF and PACF. Panel A and B show the sample autocorrelation function and partial autocorrelation function for weekly copper data over the sample period from 02/08/1993 to 30/12/2013. Both functions are evaluated up to 20 lags in line with common practice (Brigo et al., 2007).

where $\vec{r}^{\,t}_{t+1,\ldots,t+k-1}, r_{t+k}$ and $\vec{r}^{\,t+k}_{t+1,\ldots,t+k-1}$ denote the OLS estimates of r_t and r_{t+k} given the intermediate observations $r_{t+1},\ldots,r_{t+k-1}$.[22] The results of this exercise reveal that most of the commodities, where independent returns were rejected under the *LB* test, exhibit one or two significant lags, suggesting that autocorrelation may still be acceptable (Brigo et al., 2007). An exception to this conclusion is the case of crude oil, where four lags enter significantly at the 95 per cent level. A graphical representation of the analysis is given exemplarily for the case of copper in fig. 4. The test results for all other commodities are available from the author, however, as these are not of central importance and, again, similar to those presented for copper, they are omitted in the document. Given the results of the first two preliminary tests, we can draw the intermediate conclusion that the basic assumptions of stationarity and independence of returns are predominantly satisfied. In the next step we are interested in the distribution of returns. As a reference point, let us recap that the standard assumptions in GBM are log-normally distributed asset prices and, accordingly, independent, normally distributed log returns (Black & Scholes, 1973; Merton, 1976). While this assumption has been contested in equity markets by numerous authors, studies on commodity spot prices are rare.[23]

[22] The interested reader is referred to Box and Jenkins (1994) for further reference.

[23] See, for instance, Cont (2001), Schoutens (2003), Cont and Tankov (2004), Brigo et al. (2007), and Kienitz and Wetterau (2012) for studies on equity markets and Gorton and Rouwenhorst (2006) and Kat and Oomen (2007) for an

Nonetheless, all findings point in the direction that commodity returns are also not normally distributed. To ascertain the extent to which this notion is similarly supported by the dataset employed in this paper, I compute higher moments, run normality tests, and conduct a graphical study of empirical density in the remainder of this section.

As a first step, the sample mean ($\hat{\mu}$) and standard deviation ($\hat{\sigma}$) are computed for general reference and comparison with other studies such as those of Gorton and Rouwenhorst (2006) and Kat and Oomen (2007). As the calculation is standard, formulae are not reported here. To estimate the symmetry or skewness of returns, three measures are calculated. First, the most common kurtosis measure corrected for sample bias *S1* is calculated according to

$$S1 = \frac{\frac{1}{T}\sum_{t=1}^{T}(r_t-\hat{\mu})^3}{\left(\sqrt{\frac{1}{T}\sum_{t=1}^{T}(r_t-\hat{\mu})^2}\right)^3}\frac{\sqrt{T(T-1)}}{T-2}, \tag{3.2.4}$$

where T is the total number of observations in the sample. In addition to *S1*, two complementary measures *S2* and *S3* are reported. According to Kat and Oomen (2007), these are less sensitive to outliers than *S1* as they measure the asymmetry in distribution mass based on percentiles instead of third powers. The measures are computed as follows:

$$S2 = \frac{\hat{P}_{75}+\hat{P}_{25}-2\hat{P}_{50}}{\hat{P}_{75}-\hat{P}_{25}} \tag{3.2.5}$$

$$S3 = \frac{\hat{\mu}-\hat{P}_{50}}{\sum_{t=1}^{T}|r_t-\hat{P}_{50}|}T. \tag{3.2.6}$$

Besides skewness, the fourth moment, excess kurtosis, yields an indication of the concentration of returns at the centre and the tails of the distribution. It is commonly referred to as a measure of *fat-tailedness*, i.e. the extent to which extreme price swings occur more frequently than a normal distribution would imply (Kat &

analysis of commodity prices.

Oomen, 2007). Similarly to the skewness, I report the standard measure of excess kurtosis adjusted for sample bias calculated as

$$K1 = \frac{T-1}{(T-2)(T-3)}\left((T+1)\frac{\frac{1}{T}\sum_{t=1}^{T}(r_t-\hat{\mu})^4}{\left(\frac{1}{T}\sum_{t=1}^{T}(r_t-\hat{\mu})^2\right)^2} - 3(T-1)\right) \tag{3.2.7}$$

and two less outlier sensitive metrics suggested by Kat and Oomen (2007). Again, these rely on percentiles of the return series to give a measure of the relative distribution mass in the tails and the centre. These measures *K2* and *K3* are calculated as follows:

$$K2 = \frac{\hat{P}_{87.5} - \hat{P}_{62.5} + \hat{P}_{37.5} - \hat{P}_{12.5}}{\hat{P}_{75} - \hat{P}_{25}} - 1.23 \tag{3.2.8}$$

$$K3 = \frac{\hat{P}_{97.5} - \hat{P}_{2.5}}{\hat{P}_{75} - \hat{P}_{25}} - 2.91. \tag{3.2.9}$$

Turning to the results of these calculations reported in table 3, evidence is mixed in the case of skewness as some commodities exhibit positively and others negatively skewed distributions. Also, the signs of each of the three skewness measures are only consistent in six of the cases and the magnitude of skewness differs considerably. It stands out, that the highest (absolute) level of skewness is generally suggested by *S1*, reflecting the sensitivity of this measure to outliers (Kat & Oomen, 2007). To examine the impact of outliers more thoroughly, I replace *extreme* observations by the following replacement rule proposed by De Laurentis, Maino, and Molteni (2010):

$$\tilde{r}(t) = \begin{cases} Q3 + 1.5IQR & \text{if } r(t) > Q3 + 1.5IQR \\ Q1 - 1.5IQR & \text{if } r(t) < Q1 - 1.5IQR \\ r(t) & \text{else.} \end{cases} \tag{3.2.10}$$

The new, outlier adjusted return vector is denoted by $\tilde{r}$, *Q1* and *Q3* are the first and third quartile of r, respectively. The difference between *Q3* and *Q1* is the Interquar-

Table 3:

Moments of commodity returns

This table shows the first four moments of commodity returns. All indicators are calculated based on weekly data over the full sample period from 02/08/1993 to 30/12/2013. The sample mean and standard deviation are annualised with factor 52 for better comparability. All indicators are calculated based on *raw data* without any outlier treatment.

	Mean	Std. dev	S1	S2	S3	K1	K2	K3
Oil	0.09	0.38	-0.55	-0.11	-0.10	8.52	0.06	0.32
Aluminum	0.02	0.21	-0.10	0.03	0.01	3.91	0.09	0.41
Copper	0.07	0.26	-0.62	0.06	-0.01	5.57	0.14	0.81
Lead	0.09	0.33	-0.07	0.07	0.03	5.27	0.21	0.91
Nickel	0.05	0.36	0.09	0.03	0.02	5.32	0.17	0.76
Zinc	0.04	0.28	-0.46	0.04	-0.00	6.15	0.11	0.91
Gold	0.05	0.17	0.02	0.03	0.01	7.44	0.21	1.13
Silver	0.06	0.31	-0.97	0.02	-0.03	10.16	0.25	1.10
Wheat	0.02	0.30	0.20	0.06	0.06	5.20	0.11	0.70
Corn	0.03	0.32	-0.48	0.07	0.02	5.81	0.17	0.81
Soybeans	0.03	0.27	-0.68	0.05	-0.01	7.54	0.07	0.76
Sugar	0.03	0.31	-0.20	-0.02	-0.02	4.69	0.07	0.47
Coffee	0.03	0.39	0.60	-0.00	0.02	10.47	0.05	0.53
Cocoa	0.05	0.27	0.16	0.04	0.03	4.82	0.24	0.66

tile Range (IQR). The outlier adjustment leads to an average of 39 replacements across the 14 commodites or, put differently, 3.7 per cent of observations per case. If one uses a less restrictive definition of outliers based on *3IQR* instead of *1.5IQR*, the average number of replacements per case declines to 5 or 0.5 per cent. As it is difficult to judge which specification is more appropriate, we will consider the impact of both rules where helpful.

As suggested by Kat and Oomen (2007) also *S1* indicates hardly any skewness in the data after outlier replacement according to the *1.5IQR rule*. However, using *3IQR* instead, skewness remains present particularly for measure *S1*. In any case, these findings are surprising since they contradict the popular idea of commodities' positive exposure to supply shocks, which would lead us to expect a generally positive skewness throughout all cases.

Turning to the results for excess kurtosis, all metrics indicate values above normal. Even after outlier management this result is weakened, but leads to the same conclusion. This is little surprising given the extreme price swings observed in past data. To put the findings into context, crude oil, precious metals, coffee, and soybeans exhibit values for *K1* similar to the S&P 500 (K1 = 8.38).

To investigate whether the degree of skewness and excess kurtosis just identified is still consistent with normally distributed returns, two normality tests are considered next. First, the Jarque-Bera (JB) test, introduced by Jarque and Bera (1987), is a moment-based test exploiting the relationship between the *normality* of a distribution and the two higher moments *S* and *K*. The null hypothesis that a vector of returns is drawn from a normal distribution is tested against the alternative that it is subject to a different distribution. The test statistic is given by

$$JB = \frac{T}{6}\left(S^2 + \frac{(K)^2}{4}\right), \tag{3.2.11}$$

and critical values are interpolated into a table generated by Monte Carlo simulation. The second test considered was introduced by Anderson and Darling (1952) and will be referred to as the AD test. Similarly to the JB test, it assesses the null hypothesis that returns are normally distributed, however, follows a different principle so that it serves as a useful complement to the JB test. In particular, the AD test derives the empirical distribution function from the return sample under investigation and compares it to the normal cumulative distribution function. While there is a range of tests of this kind,[24] the AD test is found to be particularly powerful and sensitive to departure from normality in the tails of the distribution (Razali, 2011; Stephens, 1974). The test statistic is given by .

$$A_T^2 = -T - \sum_{t=1}^{T} \frac{2t-1}{T}\left[\ln\left(F\left(r_t\right) + \ln\left(1 - F\left(r_{T+1-t}\right)\right)\right)\right], \tag{3.2.12}$$

where $\{r_1 < \cdots < r_T\}$ are the ordered sample data points and T is the number of observations in the sample. The underlying principle of this test statistic uses a measure of total distance between the empirical and normal cumulative distribution functions evaluated at each of the ordered sample points. Critical values are also

[24] Alternatives include the Lilliefors, Kolmogorov-Smirnov and Shapiro-Wilk test (Razali, 2011).

Table 4:

Stationarity, independence, and normality of returns

All indicators are calculated based on weekly data over the full sample period from 02/08/1993 to 30/12/2013. Note that outliers have not been removed from the data.

	ADF		Ljung-Box		Jarque-Bera		Anderson-Darling	
	t	*p*	*t*	*p*	*t*	*p*	*t*	*p*
Oil	-19.00***	0.00	43.20***	0.00	1369***	0.00	7.36***	0.00
Aluminum	-31.49***	0.00	10.92	0.36	37.41***	0.00	1.85***	0.00
Copper	-30.41***	0.00	23.32***	0.01	353***	0.00	4.96***	0.00
Lead	-33.53***	0.00	9.24	0.51	224***	0.00	7.07***	0.00
Nickel	-32.29***	0.00	17.49*	0.06	233***	0.00	4.40***	0.00
Zinc	-33.68***	0.00	6.49	0.77	464***	0.00	6.92***	0.00
Gold	-33.58***	0.00	20.88**	0.02	851***	0.00	10.16***	0.00
Silver	-33.61***	0.00	15.60	0.11	2381***	0.00	10.22***	0.00
Wheat	-32.66***	0.00	5.97	0.82	215***	0.00	4.64***	0.00
Corn	-32.02***	0.00	6.96	0.73	381***	0.00	6.71***	0.00
Soybeans	-32.68***	0.00	14.02	0.17	971***	0.00	6.92***	0.00
Sugar	-31.92***	0.00	13.19	0.21	129***	0.00	3.03***	0.00
Coffee	-34.06***	0.00	25.76***	0.00	2474***	0.00	Inf***	0.00
Cocoa	-31.69***	0.00	9.63	0.47	147***	0.00	4.24***	0.00

here obtained using Monte Carlo methods. Turning to the results of these tests in table 4, we notice that normality can be rejected at the one per cent confidence level under both tests and for all commodities. This result changes for the JB test once we account for outliers according to the replacement rule introduced above. Once *extreme* values are replaced, normality can only be rejected for crude oil, but none of the other commodities. However, the selection of the outlier replacement rule is decisive also here. If one uses the less restrictive *3IQR* rule instead of *1.5IQR*, the JB test results remain unaffected compared to the case with no outlier management. Considering the AD test, the results remain entirely unaffected by outlier management regardless of the replacement rule applied. In summary, we are only able to accept the null hypothesis of normal returns under one of the two tests if a restrictive rule of so-called outlier replacement is imposed on the data, substituting 3.7 per cent of observations. This points us in the direction that returns are really not normally distributed.

As a lest step in this question, a graphical analysis may prove helpful to gain a better understanding where empirical distributions deviate from normality. In order to plot the historical distribution, kernel density estimation is a helpful tool that allows us to infer the empirical density function from independent and identically distributed random variables from a sample of observations (Parzen, 1962). This procedure is also commonly applied to asset price data[25] and, roughly speaking, draws a smooth line through the empirical sample frequencies observed at each evaluated return point (r). Accordingly, the kernel density estimate is given by

$$\hat{f}_h(r) = \frac{1}{Th}\sum_{t=1}^{T} K\left(\frac{r_t - r}{h}\right), \tag{3.2.13}$$

where $K(r)$ is the kernel function and h is the bandwidth or smoothing parameter. I follow Schoutens (2003) and use the Gaussian kernel as kernel function, which is given by

$$K(r) = \exp\left(\frac{-r^2}{2}\right)\frac{1}{\sqrt{2\pi}}. \tag{3.2.14}$$

In line with Silverman (1986), the bandwidth is calculated using the optimal rule for Gaussian data given as: $h = \sqrt[5]{4\hat{\sigma}^5/3T}$. The results of this calculation are depicted in fig. 5 for the fairly representative case of gold. In particular, the figure presents the empirical and normal density on a standard and log-scale. Additionally, panel C shows the empirical distribution quantiles plotted against the normal quantiles. In line with our previous findings, the graphical analysis verifies that in many cases commodity prices do not move as much as we would expect under a normal distribution, but at the same time we observe that the historical quantiles in the distribution tails are considerably larger than under the normal distribution. In summary, this section has shown that returns of most commodities are not normally distributed. In some cases, positive or negative skewness is a reason for this observation, however, what stands out is the considerable level of excess kurtosis common to all commodities. While skewness may be driven by a number of *ex-*

[25] See Schoutens (2003) or Kienitz and Wetterau (2012).

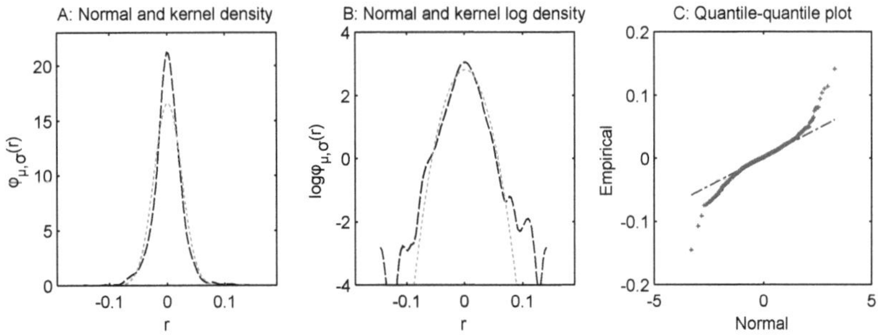

Figure 5: Kernel and normal density. The plots are generated based on weekly log returns for gold spot prices over the sample period from 02/08/1993 to 30/12/2013. Panel A shows the kernel density (black) calculated according to (3.2.13) and the normal probability density (grey) with matched weekly mean ($\mu = 0.0013$) and standard deviation ($\sigma = 0.0359$). The density is evaluated on a grid of 100 returns. Panel C shows a standard QQ plot, where the red line joins the first and third quartiles as a reference for normality.

treme observations, excess kurtosis remains present even after outliers are removed from the dataset. As a result, the hypothesis of normally distributed returns is always rejected under the distribution-based AD test and for less restrictive outlier treatment also under the JB test.

3.2.2 Jumps and GARCH effects

Given the findings of the previous subsection, we know that commodity returns are not normally distributed, most notably, due to positive excess kurtosis. In this section, the aim is to understand what factors cause these fat tails in return distributions so that we can come up with realistic stochastic processes that can mimic historical distributions. Fortunately, the list of possible ways to model fat tails and generally excess kurtosis in stochastic processes is not long. Accordingly, fat tails can be instilled into a return distribution by allowing the volatility of returns to vary stochastically (Bai, Russell, & Tiao, 2003) or by entering discontinuities, so-called jumps, into price trajectories (Brigo et al., 2007; Schoutens, 2003). In order to see which of these features is likely to work behind the scenes of commodity returns, we will consider both possibilities in some more detail hereafter.

Considering first the case of stochastic volatility, I compute standard deviations

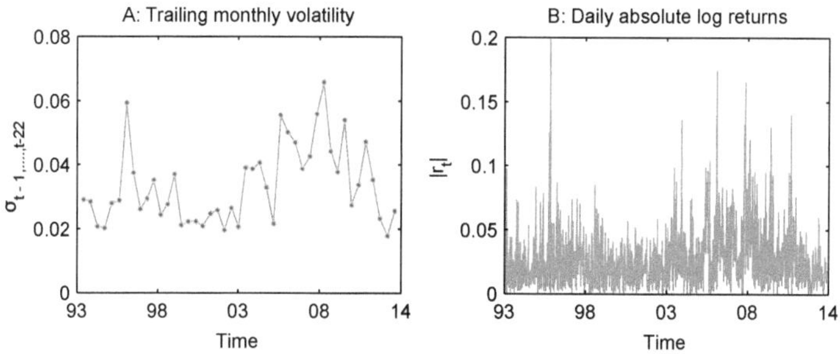

Figure 6: Time-varying volatility. Panel A depicts the standard deviation of copper log returns for trailing windows of 22 days, the equivalent of approximately one trading month. Panel B, shows the absolute values of corresponding daily log returns. Both figures are generated with sample data from 02/08/1993 to 30/12/2013.

based on daily copper data for trailing windows of one month and plot the results along with corresponding absolute weekly log returns in fig. 6. In line with the findings of Schoutens (2003) in equity markets, copper returns exhibit time-varying volatility according to panel A. Moreover, there is evidence for *volatility clusters*, i.e. a succession of periods with high or low return variance. While this observation is in so far interesting as it contradicts the standard assumption of time invariant volatility in GBM, we do not yet know to what extent it is responsible for the deviation from normality in the form of fat tails. To answer this question, I suggest to control for stochastic volatility effects and assess the resulting change in the normality of the distribution. In other words, if we find that returns are (more) normally distributed when the effect of time-varying volatility on the distribution is eliminated, we could conclude that stochastic volatility is indeed a relevant factor that can capture some of the non-normality of returns through fat tails. As a result, it may be sensible to introduce stochastic volatility also into the price models considered in section four.[26]

A useful tool for this kind of analysis are Generalised Autoregressive Conditional Heteroscedasticity (GARCH) models proposed by Engle (1982) and Bollerslev (1986). In particular, let us consider a GARCH(1,1) model where the commod-

[26]Note that a similar approach is used by Kat and Oomen (2007).

Table 5:

Stochastic volatility and normality

Al: Aluminium, Cc: Cocoa, Cf: Coffee, Cn: Corn, Co: Copper, Go: Gold, Le: Lead, Ni: Nickel, Ol: Crude oil, Si: Silver, So: Soy beans, Su: Sugar, Wt: Wheat, Zi: Zinc. Results are calculated based on weekly data over the full sample period from 02/08/1993 to 30/12/2013. Outliers were not removed prior to calculations.

	Ol	Al	Co	Le	Ni	Zi	Go	Si	Wt	Cn	So	Su	Cf	Cc
DoF_{t-fit}	4.75	8.60	5.12	4.10	5.03	4.21	3.52	3.68	5.11	4.25	4.35	5.97	5.07	5.35
DoF_{GARCH}	6.91	12.57	7.70	7.30	6.12	7.21	5.36	5.25	5.85	4.87	5.86	7.48	7.57	5.49
ΔAD	0.46	0.46	0.43	0.3	0.66	0.32	0.41	0.47	0.75	0.75	0.53	0.62	0.43	0.95
$\gamma = \alpha + \beta$	0.97	0.99	0.96	1.00	0.99	1.00	1.00	0.99	0.97	0.92	0.93	0.99	0.96	1.00

ity log return is represented as the following stationary variance process: $r_t = \varepsilon_t$, where $\varepsilon_t = \sigma_t z_t$ and z_t is a white noise process as discussed earlier in this section. σ_t^2 is a conditional variance process given by

$$\sigma_t^2 = \kappa + \alpha_1 \varepsilon_{t-1}^2 + \beta_1 \sigma_{t-1}^2 \qquad \alpha_1 + \beta_1 < 1. \tag{3.2.15}$$

This model is fitted to the historical series of returns using MLE and letting the innovations follow Student's t-distribution. Now, recap that this distribution has fat tails for a low number of Degrees of Freedom (DoF) and approaches the normal distribution if DoF is increased. If, therefore, the fitted GARCH(1,1) model implies a high number of DoF in the distribution of innovations, we can conclude that returns are close to normally distributed once it has been accounted for the impact of varying volatility. If, furthermore, DoF are lower if a Student's t-distribution is fitted to the return data without controlling for stochastic volatility, we also have a reference for the relative importance of stochastic volatility for each commodity. On the contrary, if DoF do not rise at all once GARCH effects are controlled, we can infer that the effort to include stochastic volatility in a price model is probably not worthwhile.

The results of this calculation are presented in table 5. For all commodities, the number of DoF in the Student's t-distribution increases if we account for GARCH effects vis-à-vis the case where a stand-alone t-distribution is fitted to past returns without taking the effect of stochastic volatility into account. Although, this is already the insight we were looking for, it is somewhat difficult to judge the relative extent to which the non-normality of returns can be explained by GARCH effects so far. Recap that the t-distribution becomes asymptotically more normal for higher DoF in the sense that, for instance, an increase of DoF from one to two has a much larger impact on the similarity between the t-distribution and the Gaussian distribution than an increase from 99 to 100. Thus, the absolute change in DoF is of little use. To make the relative importance of stochastic volatility for each commodity more transparent, I propose ΔAD as a measure to quantify the change in *total distance* between the two distributions before and after GARCH effects are controlled. It is calculated according to (3.2.16) and shown in table 5.

$$\Delta AD = \frac{\int_{-\infty}^{\infty} |F_{N(0,1)}(x) - F_{t(0,1,\nu^{GARCH})}(x)|dx}{\int_{-\infty}^{\infty} |F_{N(0,1)}(x) - F_{t(0,1,\nu^{fit})}(x)|dx}, \tag{3.2.16}$$

$F_{N(0,1)}$ denotes the cumulative standard normal distribution function, $F_{t(0,1,\nu^{GARCH})}$ refers to the t-distribution's cumulative distribution function with DoF retrieved from the fitted GARCH model, and $F_{t(0,1,\nu^{fit})}$ denotes the same distribution function, however, the number of DoF is obtained from the best MLE fit to historical returns without accounting for GARCH effects. Please note that the integrals are numerically approximated with the trapezoid rule over the interval [-1000 1000]. The result of ΔAD will lie in the interval [0 1], where a value of zero indicates that stochastic volatility is entirely responsible for the non-normality of returns and one indicates that it has no impact on normality. If $0 < \Delta AD < 1$, stochastic volatility can account for some but not all the non-normality of a return distribution.

The calculation of this measure indicates that the distance between the t-distribution and normal distribution declines by more then 50% in the majority of cases. Particularly, in the case of lead and zinc stochastic volatility has a strong influence on return distributions, but seems to be of low importance in the case of cocoa. These findings are perfectly in line with those of Kat and Oomen (2007), who similarly find low conditional kurtosis in cocoa and persistent fat tails in a range of other commodities.

For the purpose of completeness and general interest, I also report the sum of the lag coefficients ($\gamma = \alpha_1 + \beta_1$) of the conditional volatility process. Similarly to our earlier discussion of the autoregressive coefficient in the AR(1) process, γ provides an indication of the persistence of volatility shocks. As γ has values above 0.9 throughout, we can infer that if volatility increases (decreases), it is likely to stay high (low) for some time (Kat & Oomen, 2007). This is consistent with the previous observation of volatility clusters in fig. 6.

Having analysed the relation between stochastic volatility and excess kurtosis, it is natural to investigate whether there is evidence that the second source of excess kurtosis, jumps in prices, is additionally present in commodity return data. First, to gain a better understanding of this concept, I provide an illustrative price path with jumps in fig. 7. This path is right continuous, describing the property that if a jump occurs at time t, the asset price S_t includes this jump. As a result, the jump produces a discontinuity in the price trajectory of S from the left. Put differently, there is no chance at time $t^- = t - \Delta t$ to unveil the uncertainty about the occurrence of the subsequent jump in point t. This behaviour of a price path corresponds to sudden, unexpected arrivals of important information upon, which traders change their opinion on the value of a commodity (Merton, 1976). This type of large shock has to be distinguished from the many small shocks that are due to e.g. the arrival of less important information or minor supply and demand imbalances, which cause marginal changes in the asset price. In order to test for the existence of shocks, I apply the *spectographic* analysis proposed by Ait-Sahalia and Jacod (2012). While this test is devised for the application to high frequency data, I show graphically that it is also useful to gain some basic insights about the empirical jumpiness of commodity prices measured at a lower frequency. Although, a detailed explanation of the test method is beyond the scope of this paper, let us briefly consider the general principle.

For any historical series of n asset prices (S) over the interval [0 T], we can observe discrete price changes $\Delta S(t) = S(t) - S(t-1)$ for each observation t.

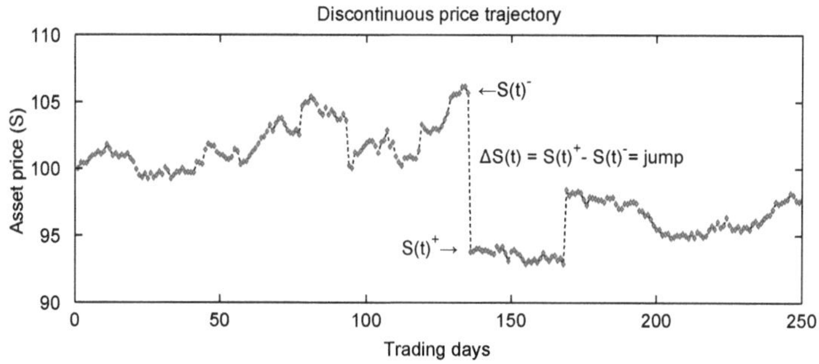

Figure 7: Discontinuous price trajectory. This graph depicts a price path generated with the jump diffusion model proposed by Merton (1976) based on the following parameters: Initial asset price = 100, risk free interest rate = 0.05, time horizon = 1 year, volatility = 0.05, volatility of jumps = 0.05, mean of jumps = 0, jump intensity = 10, discretisation steps = 250. A more detailed explanation of this model is given in section 4.1.3 of this paper.

These are to be contrasted with the actual, unobservable jumps of S denoted as $\Delta S = S(t) - S(t)^-$, where $S(t)^-$ is the asset price one infinitesimally small quantity of time before the jump occurs. Now, we assume that the stochastic data generating process of p is an Itô semimartingale.[27] A semimartingale can be decomposed into the sum of a drift, a continuous Brownian-motion part, and a discontinuous jump part. More formally we can write

$$S_t = S_0 + \underbrace{\int_0^t b_s ds}_{\text{drift}} + \underbrace{\int_0^t \sigma_s dW_s}_{\text{Brownian part}} + \underbrace{\int_0^t \int_{\{|x| \leq \varepsilon\}} x(\mu - \nu)(ds, dx)}_{\text{small jumps}} \tag{3.2.17}$$

$$+ \underbrace{\int_0^t \int_{\{|x| > \varepsilon\}} x\mu(ds, dx)}_{\text{big jumps}},$$

where μ is the jump measure of S and its predictable compensator is the Lévy measure ν.[28] The distinction between small and big jumps (x) according to the threshold ε is arbitrary, but fixed. To learn which of the different components of the semimartingale are necessary to produce the historical returns and what their

[27] See Cont and Tankov (2004) or Björk (2009) for further reference.

[28] The jump compensator ensures that the process remains a martingale in the presence of jumps (Battauz & Ortu, 2009; Björk, 2009). A more detailed discussion on martingales and risk-neutrality is given in section four.

relative importance is, the following measurement device is used:

$$B(k, u_n, \Delta_n) = \sum_{i=1}^{T/\Delta_n} |\Delta_i^n S|^k 1_{\{|\Delta_i^n S| \leq u_n\}}. \tag{3.2.18}$$

The quantity B is computed for different powers (k), truncation levels (u), and sampling frequencies (Δ). For instance, the authors explain that powers of $k < 2$, will put more emphasis on the continuous component of the process, while $k > 2$ will accentuate the jump parts. Truncating the increments at u_n to exclude e.g. large or small increments ((3.2.18) is changed accordingly) enables us to extract information on different types of jumps. Besides, adjustments in sampled return frequencies Δ_n help to distinguish whether variations converge to a finite limit, to zero, or diverge to infinity so that inferences can be made about which component of the semimartingale dominates at a particular power. Based on these different computations, a number of test statistics can be computed, which indicate the presence of jumps (S_j), the degree of jump activity (S_{FA}), the presence of continuous Brownian motion (S_w), and the relative magnitude of variation in S that is attributable to a jump or Brownian component (QV_{Split}).[29] As the test is originally developed for high frequency data, whereas we are interested in price behaviour on a daily (or lower) frequency, I decide to show the test statistics not only for daily historical commodity returns but also for a corresponding jump diffusion price path similar to the one presented in fig. 7. As we know the properties of the jump diffusion path, it is clear that the test should expose both, the jump and diffusion component, so that we get a better feeling for the overall reliability of the results in our *low frequency* context. Fig. 8 shows the results for both, the jump diffusion test path and the exemplary and representative case of coffee. Please note that, again, the other test results are available from the author, however, since little additional insights would result and in order not to exaggerate the length of this document, a presentation is omitted. Turning to the findings, we may notice first that the test

[29] Please see Ait-Sahalia and Jacod (2012) for further explanation. Implementation details and sample code are available from `http://www.princeton.edu/~yacine/research`.

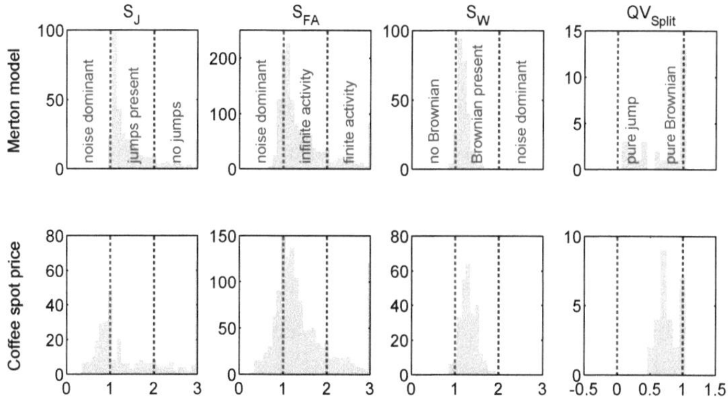

Figure 8: Spectographic jump test. The four columns of the plot refer to the four test statistics of the spectographic jump test. S_j: Presence of jumps, S_{FA}: Degree of jump activity, S_w: Presence of a Brownian motion, QV_{Split}: Relative importance of jump and Brownian component. The top four plots refer to the Merton jump diffusion model as a benchmark and reference point. The bottom four plots refer to the daily coffee spot price sampled over the period: 02/08/1993 - 30/12/2013. Note that daily data is used instead of weekly prices as the interpretation of jumps at such low frequency is problematic (Ait-Sahalia & Jacod, 2012).

results are in line with expectations for the test path. In particular, the presence of jumps is confirmed, there is evidence for infinite activity jumps (small Brownian increments), finite activity jumps (irregular large jumps from the compound Poisson process)[30], the presence of a Brownian motion or diffusion component is confirmed, and, lastly, we see that the variations in S are caused by both a jump and Brownian process. In the case of coffee, we may notice some evidence for the presence of jumps, however, the relative importance of the Brownian component is clearly higher than under the stylised model path. As these findings are almost perfectly representative for all other commodities in the sample, we can conclude that jumps, although not as clearly as stochastic volatility, may need to be considered in commodity price modelling to mimic the fat tails of historical return distributions.

[30]As mentioned previously, a more detailed explanation of the Merton model is postponed to section four. For further reference see Merton (1976).

4 Modelling commodity prices

On the basis of the previous statistical findings, it is the objective of this section to propose models for the stochastic simulation of commodity prices that are theoretically consistent with empirical data. In this regard, recap that mean reversion cannot generally be proven in past prices over the last two decades. Even if a much longer time horizon would allow us to reject a unit root in prices, we concluded that the statistical properties of mean reversion seem to neither fit reality over the recent past (as shown by the backtest in fig. 3) nor the future outlook of uncertain and persistently volatile commodity markets. It has also been identified that past returns are not normally distributed, most notably, due to excess kurtosis and that time-varying volatility and jumps in price trajectories are both possible causes for non-normality. As discussed in section one of this thesis, the most common stochastic processes in real options applications assume either mean reversion of prices or normally distributed returns. Hence, we will assess the merits of alternative price processes that have already found widespread application in pricing equity and fixed income derivatives also in the case of commodity prices. In this sense, I follow Brooks and Prokopczuk (2013), who similarly draw on the often more developed and broad literature on equity derivatives pricing and transfer concepts such as stochastic volatility models to commodity markets. The remainder of this section is organised as follows. In the first half, the popular case of GBM is considered as a reference point and convenient example to clarify some fundamental concepts of stochastic calculus and risk-neutral simulation in Monte Carlo-based valuation. Thereafter, we will step-by-step relax some of the restrictive assumptions of GBM on the normality of returns, constant volatility, and continuous price trajectories by introducing theoretically more realistic stochastic processes in the following subsections. In the second half of this section, each process is evaluated in terms of goodness of fit to past commodity time series so that first conclusions can be drawn on the relative appropriateness of different models.

4.1 Stochastic processes

The idea to describe asset prices in a speculative market using a stochastic process[31] was first proposed by Bachelier (1900), but gained little attention until the 1950s when empirical studies revealed that serial correlation of asset price returns was negligible (Mantegna & Stanley, 2000) and the Efficient Market Hypothesis (EMH) was postulated by Samuelson (1964). Since then, various stochastic processes have been suggested for different applications. Simple examples of a stochastic process include, for instance, the RW and AR process as well as GBM, the Vasicek, or the Merton model we have already touched upon peripherally in the context of empirical data analysis. In this part of the paper, we will focus more explicitly on stochastic processes for commodity price simulation. To begin with, a more detailed analysis of GBM is given – a process that the reader will be familiar with already. The reason for this choice of a starting point is twofold. First, it has already been mentioned that GBM is a popular model in the context of real options applications so that the relative performance of this process to others may be of general interest. Second, GBM lends itself to the preliminary study of some central concepts in stochastic calculus and Monte Carlo simulation without exaggerated complexity. In particular, it is useful at this stage to elaborate on three topics in more detail upfront. First, the continuous time representation of a stochastic process in the form of its Stochastic Differential Equation (SDE). Second, how to solve the SDE via stochastic calculus in order to simulate the process on a discrete time grid of days, weeks, or months. Third, the difference between process simulation under the historical probability measure $\mathbb{P}$ and the risk-neutral probability measure $\mathbb{Q}$, which is later required for the valuation of contingent claims.

Let us first consider the continuous time representation of GBM. Accordingly, the

[31] A stochastic process can be defined as a sequence of chronologically ordered random variables $\{P_t; t \geq 0\}$ (Franke et al., 2011). See also Schoutens (2003) and Björk (2009) for additional reference.

asset price S is governed by the expression

$$S(t) = S(0) + \int_0^t S(s)\mu ds + \int_0^t S(s)\sigma dW^{\mathbb{P}}(s), \tag{4.1.1}$$

where μ refers to the drift or instantaneous rate of return of S, σ denotes (constant) volatility, and $dW^{\mathbb{P}}$ is a standard Brownian motion under the historical or *real world* probability measure $\mathbb{P}$ with respect to the information structure or filtration $\mathbb{F}$. In other words, $dW^{\mathbb{P}}$ can be interpreted as the previously discussed white noise process or simply a normally distributed disturbance term that is independent of everything that has happened up to time t.[32] While this continuous time representation is an elegant building block for derivative pricing formulae such as the Black-Scholes model, we rarely encounter real options that admit closed form, continuous time solutions. As a result, we either need to approximate GBM in a lattice framework or rely on Monte Carlo simulation of the adequately discretised process.[33] As the Monte Carlo-based approach will prove most flexible for our purposes of comparing different processes, for which no lattice representation may be available, we need to discretise (4.1.1). This brings us to the second main question we want to answer in this introductory section, namely, how to solve the SDE for a discrete price path.

Many stochastic processes do not admit an exact closed form solution to their SDE and need to be solved via some approximative discretisation scheme.[34] This is not the case with GBM. However, the presence of an integral with respect to $dW^{\mathbb{P}}(s)$ prevents us, from using the usual rules of differential calculus (Battauz & Ortu, 2009). Instead, we can first write (4.1.1) in short notation as:

$$dS(t) = \mu S(t)dt + \sigma S(t)dW(t). \tag{4.1.2}$$

[32] See Björk (2009) for the formal requirements that must hold for W to be a Brownian motion.

[33] See Cox et al. (1979) for technical reference on lattice approximation, Trigeorgis (1996) or Copeland and Antikarov (2003) for lattice-based real option valuation, and Tsekrekos et al. (2012) or Yungchih Wang (2011) for the application of Monte Carlo simulation in investment valuation.

[34] Common schemes include the Euler, Predictor-Corrector, or Milstein scheme. See Kienitz and Wetterau (2012) for further reference.

According to Björk (2009), we can apply Itô's formula to this type of stochastic differential. Accordingly we need to compute

$$df(t,S(t)) = \left\{\frac{\delta f}{\delta t} + \mu\frac{\delta f}{\delta S} + \frac{1}{2}\sigma^2\frac{\delta^2 f}{\delta S^2}\right\}dt + \sigma\frac{\delta f}{\delta S}dW^{\mathbb{P}}. \quad (4.1.3)$$

In line with the assumptions of GBM we set $f(t,S) = \ln S$ and compute the respective differentials as:

$$\frac{\delta f}{\delta t} = 0,\ \frac{\delta f}{\delta S} = \frac{1}{S},\ \frac{\delta^2 f}{\delta S^2} = -\frac{1}{S^2}.$$

Substituting these into (4.1.3) and reversely substituting $f(t,S) = \ln S$ yields:

$$\ln\left(\frac{S(t)}{S(t-1)}\right) = \left[\mu\frac{1}{S}S + \frac{1}{2}\sigma^2\left(-\frac{1}{S^2}\right)S^2\right] + \sigma\frac{1}{S}SdW^{\mathbb{P}}. \quad (4.1.4)$$

Exponentiating and writing the result in terms of t as opposed to dt, we get

$$S(t) = S(0)\exp\left[\left(\mu - \frac{1}{2}\sigma^2\right)t + \sigma W^{\mathbb{P}}(t)\right], \quad (4.1.5)$$

which is the familiar GBM representation in discrete time. Although, this formulation allows to simulate stochastic price trajectories under the *real world* probability measure, it does not yet allow us to price derivatives in a Monte Carlo framework. This leads to the third question of how to simulate prices in the risk-neutral Monte Carlo-based valuation of contingent claims.

Intuitively, we know from the findings of Cox et al. (1979) that the possibility of creating a replicating portfolio allows the option writer to eliminate all risk arising from the uncertain movement of the underlying asset, on which the derivative is written. While this logic allows to pin down the value of the option, it also implies that in a risk-neutral world all assets would earn the risk-free rate of interest since risk-neutral investors would not demand a higher rate of return for holding risky assets (Glasserman, 2003). As a result, it is intuitive that contingent claims valuation using the Monte Carlo method will require us to simulate asset prices in such a way that the simulated asset return corresponds in expectation to the risk-free interest rate. More formally, we require an equivalent probability measure $\mathbb{Q}$ such that under this new measure all discounted risky asset prices become martingales in expectation[35] such that

$$\mathbb{E}_t^{\mathbb{Q}} = \left[\frac{S(t+1)}{B(t+1)}\right] = \frac{S(t)}{B(t)}, \quad \forall t \tag{4.1.6}$$

where $B(t) = \exp(rt)$ is a continuously compounded bond with a value of one and r the risk-free rate of interest (Battauz & Ortu, 2009). Roughly speaking, we are trying to adjust the measure, under which we formulate expectations on future asset prices in such a way that an otherwise risky security yields a return equal to the risk-free rate of interest in expectation. By the Girsanov Theorem, it can be shown that the existence of such a probability measure $\mathbb{Q}$ is equivalent to the existence of a market price of risk process given by: $\nu = (\mu - r)/\sigma$.[36] Now, with reference to (4.1.5), it should hold that $W^{\mathbb{Q}} = W^{\mathbb{P}} + \nu t$. To obtain the risk-neutral representation of the process, we can substitute $\mu = r + \sigma\nu$ and collect terms in the exponent of (4.1.5) to obtain

$$\begin{aligned}\left(r + \sigma\nu - \frac{1}{2}\sigma^2\right)t + \sigma dW^{\mathbb{P}}(t) &= \left(r - \frac{1}{2}\sigma^2\right)t + \sigma\left(dW^{\mathbb{P}}(t) + \nu t\right)\\ &= \left(r - \frac{1}{2}\sigma^2\right)t + \sigma dW^{\mathbb{Q}}(t).\end{aligned}$$

Replacing the exponent of (4.1.5) with this result, we see that our earlier intuition that an asset should yield the risk-free rate in the risk-neutral setting is confirmed.[37] To put this result into context, we can value a typical European call option derivative by simulating an appropriate number of price paths (or only the prices relevant to compute the payoffs) under the risk-neutral measure, calculate the terminal

[35]See, for instance, Mantegna and Stanley (2000) or Björk (2009) for further reference on martingale theory.

[36]Note that under the existence of this process, the usual no-arbitrage assumption holds and the market is said to be complete if this process can be uniquely determined (Schoutens, 2003).

[37]Please note that in the remainder of this section, the superscripts for the historical and risk-neutral probability measure are omitted for notational convenience.

payoffs, discount them to the present at the risk-free interest rate, and obtain a valuation by taking the average across paths (Battauz & Ortu, 2009). Note that in the presence of a convenience yield or storage costs, these have to be subtracted from the risk-free interest rate in the drift term (Glasserman, 2003).[38] What remains to be considered, according to the logic adopted in the next subsections, is a sensitivity analysis of asset price paths and the return distribution with respect to changes in the input parameters μ and σ. Since, however, this exercise would add little new insights in the case of GBM, the analysis is omitted.

In summary, note that while it took us some time to go through the solution of the SDE and the concept of risk-neutral simulation for a Monte Carlo setting, these considerations are to a large extent valid for the more complex stochastic processes presented next. Even if exact solutions to the SDEs are not available in some cases and require the use of some discretisation scheme, the idea of solving the SDE to work in discrete time remains unchanged. This logic applies equally to the martingale correction, which is, in many cases, more difficult to derive than for GBM, but is intuitively equivalent. As a result, I will omit lengthy derivations in the following three subsections to focus more on intuition, application, and those formulae directly relevant to obtain final results.

4.1.1 Stochastic volatility

Earlier, we concluded that the volatility of commodity returns is not constant and that it accounts for fat tails in the distribution of returns. As Pindyck (1999) suggests that "the GBM assumption will be appropriate only if [...] volatility is relatively constant" (p. 24), it seems worthwhile to allow volatility to follow a stochastic process itself. A popular model for this purpose is the one proposed by Heston (1993), which has already been successfully applied to commodity markets by Brooks and Prokopczuk (2013). The model is characterised by the following set

[38]For the possibility of return shortfall, applying in some cases to non-traded capital investments, please refer to Tsekrekos et al. (2012) for further reference.

of SDEs:

$$dS(t) = \mu S(t)\,dt + \sqrt{V(t)}S(t)\,dW_1(t) \tag{4.1.7}$$
$$dV(t) = \kappa(\Theta - V(t))\,dt + \nu\sqrt{V(t)}dW_2(t)$$
$$\langle dW_1, dW_2\rangle = \rho dt.$$

In line with previous notation, S is the asset price, V the variance process, Θ the long-term variance, ν the volatility of variance, and ρ the correlation between the Brownian motions W_1 and W_2, which allow us to model the commonly observed relationship between volatility and asset prices.[39]

In order to simulate the Heston process in discrete time, we cannot solve the SDE by stochastic calculus as we did in the case of GBM. Instead, a number of sampling schemes have been proposed. As the exact scheme introduced by Broadie and Kaya (2006) is computationally expensive, I use the Quadratic Exponential scheme of Andersen (2008) as described by Kienitz and Wetterau (2012). Since the analytic representation of the QE scheme is somewhat lengthy and of little intuitive interest, please refer to appendix B4 for details.

More interesting in our context, however, is the probability density of returns implied by the model. This will be used for later model calibration and helps us to understand exactly how the value of each input parameter affects the shape of the return distribution. As the probability density is not given explicitly, we have to compute it from the model's characteristic function via the fast Fourier transform algorithm (see appendix B3). The characteristic function is obtained from Kienitz and Wetterau (2012) and can be written as follows: [40]

$$\varphi_{Heston}(u,t) = \exp\left(A_H(u,t) + B_\sigma(u,t)V(t) + iuX(t)\right) \tag{4.1.8}$$

[39] See, for instance, Schoutens (2003) for the case of equity markets and Richter and Sörensen (2003) for commodities.

[40] For further reference on characteristic functions in the context of stochastic processes see Schoutens (2003) and Cont and Tankov (2004).

$$A_H(u,t) = \frac{\kappa\Theta}{\nu^2}\left[(\kappa-\rho\nu ui - D)t - 2\log\left(\frac{G\exp(-Dt)}{G-1} - 1\right)\right]$$

$$B_\sigma(u,t) = \frac{\kappa-\rho\nu ui - D}{\omega^2}\left[\frac{1-\exp(-Dt)}{1-G\exp(-Dt)}\right]$$

$$G = \frac{\kappa-\rho\nu ui - D}{\kappa-\rho\nu ui + D}$$

$$D = \sqrt{(\kappa-\rho\nu ui)^2 + u(i+u)\nu^2}.$$

With respect to notation, u refers to an appropriate grid of values, for which the function is evaluated and i is the imaginary unit from complex numbers theory. The relation between model inputs, the distribution of returns, and sample paths for the price process are shown in fig. 9. As we would expect, higher levels of Θ lead to a wider distribution of returns, a more volatile asset price path, and, by definition, a higher level of long-term variance. Considering the mean reversion speed of the variance to its long-term level (κ), we see first that we obtain a peaked distribution for low values. This is intuitive since we have set Θ greater than the initial variance. For a low κ, the variance remains low for a longer time, leading to more returns clustered around the centre of the distribution. This logic is confirmed by the asset price and variance paths. The interpretation of the volatility of variance (ν) is less straightforward, but offers, in any case, another lever to control the overall level of volatility (Kienitz & Wetterau, 2012). Eventually, the correlation between asset prices and volatility (ρ) allows to control the skewness of the return distribution.

4.1.2 Jump diffusion

Following from the study of jumps in commodity prices, another potentially fruitful direction to pursue is the use of diffusion processes similar to GBM, but augmented by a jump component. In this section, we will consider two processes of this kind. First, the classical jump diffusion process by Merton (1976), which we have already used as a benchmark to judge the reliability of the test for the presence of jumps in past prices. Second, the model by Bates (1996), which can be seen as

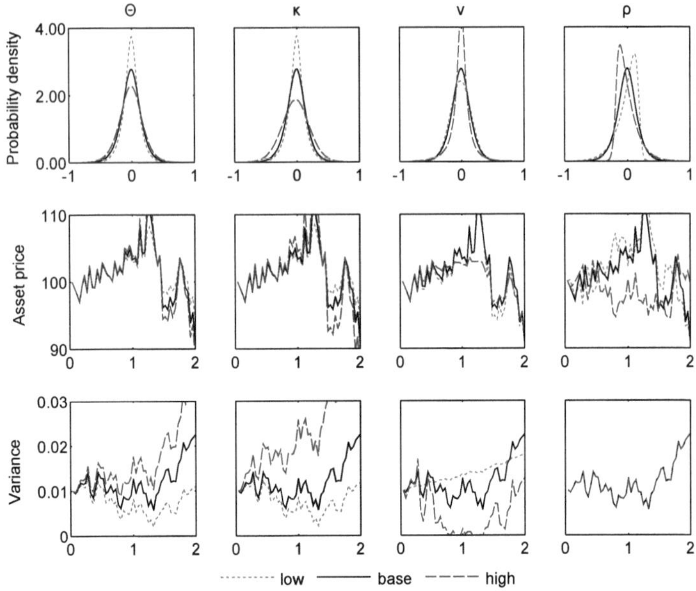

Figure 9: The Heston model: Parameter sensitivities. $T = 2$, $S(0) = 100$, $V(0) = 0.01$, $\Theta = 0.005, 0.05, 0.1$, $\kappa = 0.001, 0.1, 0.5$, $\nu = 0.01, 0.1, 0.25$, $\rho = -0.9, 0, 0.9$. The base case refers to the central value in the previously specified ranges. If the sensitivity of output is evaluated with respect to one of the (four) variables under consideration, all other parameters will be set to the base case value. Note that all paths are calculated based on the same pseudo random number stream and are calculated under the physical probability measure $\mathbb{P}$. Densities are evaluated on a grid of 1000 points.

a combination of the Heston and Merton model allowing for stochastic volatility and jumps.

Under the Merton model, price dynamics are governed by the following set of equations:

$$dS(t) = \mu S(t)\,dt + \sigma S(t)\,dW(t) + S(t)(Y-1)\,dN(t) \tag{4.1.9}$$

$$Y = \mu_J \exp\left(-\frac{1}{2}\sigma_J^2 + \sigma_J z\right), \quad z \sim \mathcal{N}(0,1).$$

The parameters μ and σ correspond to the drift and volatility as in the Black-Scholes model. Y governs the log-normal jump size distribution, with mean jump size μ_J and volatility of jump size σ_J. $N(t)$ is a Poisson process, determining the random occurrences of jumps with intensity λ. By Itô's formula for jump diffusions, we can solve for the discrete representation of the process in a similar way as for GBM and get

$$S(t) = S(0)\exp\left(\mu - \frac{1}{2}\sigma^2\right)t + \sigma W(t)\left(\prod_{j=1}^{N(t)} Y_j\right). \tag{4.1.10}$$

Kienitz and Wetterau (2012) show that setting the drift to

$$r - q - \frac{\sigma^2}{2} - \lambda\left(e^{-\frac{\sigma_J^2}{2} - \mu_J} - 1\right), \tag{4.1.11}$$

yields a martingale to simulate the process under risk-neutral dynamics for the application in Monte Carlo-based valuation.
As in the Heston model, we have to compute the return density for the Merton process from its characteristic function, which is given by:

$$\varphi_{Merton}(u) = \exp\left[i\mu ut - \frac{\sigma^2 u}{2}t + \lambda t\left(e^{i\mu_J u - \frac{1}{2\sigma_J^2 u^2}} - 1\right)\right]. \tag{4.1.12}$$

As we would expect, this is just the simplified product of the characteristic function from the normal distribution (for the Black-Scholes or GBM part of the process) and the logarithmic jump part. To see now the impact of different parameters on the return distribution and price paths, let us turn to fig. 9. As in the case of GBM, we skip the consideration of parameters μ and σ. The jump mean controls the skewness of the distribution. This is sensible as we would, for instance, expect the return distribution to show more probability mass around the left tail if the jumps have on average negative values. The volatility of jumps controls the peakedness of the distribution. Little volatility results in few extreme observations and a concentration of probability around the centre of the distribution. Finally, the effect of jump intensity is similar to jump volatility. If fewer jumps occur, the number of extreme observations decreases so that returns cluster around the centre.

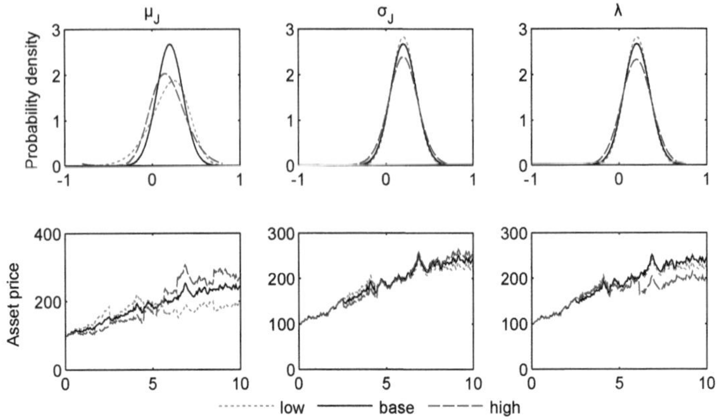

Figure 10: The Merton model: Parameter sensitivities. $T = 10$, $S(0) = 100$, $\mu = 0.1$, $\sigma = 0.1$, $\mu_J = -0.15, 0, 0.15$, $\sigma_J = 0.001, 0.05, 0.1$, $\lambda = 0.01, 0.5, 2$. See footnote of fig. 9 for more details.

We have seen that the incorporation of volatility or jumps in a stochastic process offers more control over the shape of return distributions and the dynamics of price paths. Thus, it may be useful to take this idea one step further. In particular, the Bates model can be seen as a Heston model with the addition of log-normal jumps from the Merton process. While the process was originally motivated by the desire to model smiles in the implied volatility surface even for short-dated financial options (Kienitz & Wetterau, 2012), we will investigate whether the additional parameters also lead to a better model fit to past return data. According to Bates (1996), the SDE governing the evolution of this process is given by

$$
\begin{aligned}
dS(t) &= \mu S(t)\,dt + \sqrt{V(t)}S(t)\,dW_1(t) + (Y-1)\,S(t)\,dN(t) \qquad (4.1.13)\\
dV(t) &= \kappa(\Theta - V(t))\,dt + \nu\sqrt{V(t)}\,dW_2(t)\\
\langle dW_1, dW_2\rangle &= \rho dt.
\end{aligned}
$$

With respect to notation, we notice immediately the similarity to the Heston process and the additional jump part inherited from the Merton model. For the discretisation of the Bates model, I use the Quadratic Exponential scheme known from the Heston model but, augmented for jumps as described by Kienitz and Wetterau (2012). What remains to be discussed is the distribution of returns. To this end, Kienitz and Wetterau (2012) show that the characteristic function of the Bates process is given by

$$\varphi_{Bates} = \varphi_{Heston} \cdot \exp\left(\lambda t\left(-\mu_J iu + \exp\left(A\right) - 1\right)\right) \tag{4.1.14}$$
$$A = iu\, log\left(1 + \mu_J\right) + \frac{1}{2}\sigma_J^2 iu\left(iu - 1\right).$$

The first part of (4.1.14) is just the characteristic function from the Heston model and the second part the characteristic function of the log-normal jump part from the Merton model we have seen earlier in simplified form. Since we have already analysed the sensitivities of all parameters of the Bates model separately for the Heston and Merton process, this part is skipped here to avoid duplication of work.

4.1.3 Lévy processes

One common characteristic of the previously considered processes is the presence of a Brownian motion W which affects the price process continuously. Even when jumps were added, we only introduced some irregular discontinuities in otherwise continuous price trajectories. Another class of models that does not necessarily contain a Brownian part is known as *exponential Lévy models*, in honour of Paul Lévy, the pioneer of the concept (Schoutens, 2003). These processes are pure jump models based on infinitely divisible Lévy distributions instead of the Gaussian normal distribution. Similarly to Brownian motion based processes, Lévy models have independent and stationary increments, but are more flexible than models based on the normal distribution in the way they can account for skewness and kurtosis of returns (Cont & Tankov, 2004). For this reason, it may be worthwhile to study the applicability of such models in commodity markets and real option valuation. While the array of popular Lévy processes is long,[41] we will study the

[41]See Schoutens (2003) and the sources cited therein for a more comprehensive overview of Lévy processes.

Variance Gamma (VG) process by Madan and Seneta (1990) and Boyarchenko and Levendorskii (as cited in Kienitz & Wetterau, 2012), the Normal Inverse Gaussian (NIG) process, and the NIG process with stochastic clock governed by a Cox-Ingersoll-Ross (CIR) process as outlined by Schoutens (2003) and Kienitz and Wetterau (2012).[42]

Beginning with the VG process, we can choose between two representations. First, the process can be expressed as the difference between two Gamma processes $U(t)$ and $D(t)$ so that $S(t) := U(t) - D(t)$. Alternatively, we can follow Brigo et al. (2007) and represent the VG process as a time-changed Brownian motion.[43] For notational convenience, we pursue the latter of the two possibilities and write

$$S(t) = \mu S(t)\,dt + \theta dg(t) + \sigma dW(g(t)), \tag{4.1.15}$$

where the difference to the earlier considered SDE of GBM lies in the term $g(t)$, which characterises *market activity time* (Brigo et al., 2007). More specifically, market time is assumed to follow an increasing random process with stationary increments that reconciles with calendar time on average over a given time span. This process is driven by random variables drawn from a gamma distribution as follows: $\{g(t)\} \sim \Gamma(t/\nu, \nu)$. Given the SDE of the VG process and knowing the solution to the GBM SDE, it is intuitive that the solution to (4.1.15) in discrete time and under the historical probability measure is given by

$$S(t) = S(0)\exp\left[\mu dt + \theta g(t) + \sigma\sqrt{g(t)}W(t)\right]. \tag{4.1.16}$$

In order to obtain risk-neutrality, Kienitz and Wetterau (2012) show that we need to replace the historical drift measure μ by the expression

$$\mu = r - \frac{1}{\nu}\log\left(1 - \theta\nu - \nu\frac{\sigma^2}{2}\right), \tag{4.1.17}$$

[42] See Cox, Ingersoll, and Ross (1985) for details on the stand-alone CIR process.

[43] For further reference on Brownian subordination see Cont and Tankov (2004).

where r denotes the risk-free interest rate as usual. For the probability density of returns, the VG process admits an explicit solution, taken from Brigo et al. (2007). Accordingly we can calculate

$$f_{VG}(x) = \frac{2e^{\frac{\theta(x-\mu)}{\sigma^2}}}{\sigma\sqrt{2\pi}\nu^{\frac{t}{\nu}}\Gamma\left(\frac{1}{\nu}\right)}\left(\frac{|x-\mu|}{\sqrt{\frac{2\sigma^2}{\nu}+\theta^2}}\right)^{\frac{t}{\nu}-\frac{1}{2}} K_{\frac{t}{\nu}-\frac{1}{2}}\left(\frac{|x-\mu|\sqrt{\frac{2\sigma^2}{\nu}+\theta^2}}{\sigma^2}\right), \tag{4.1.18}$$

where x refers to a grid of returns, where the density is evaluated, and $K_\eta(\cdot)$ is a modified Bessel function of the third kind with index η specified in the subscript of K in (4.1.18). To understand how the input parameters affect returns and price trajectories, fig. 11 provides the usual overview. Note that according to Brigo et al. (2007), μ and σ play an identical role in the VG process and GBM so that we can omit the analysis of these parameters also here. The results show that

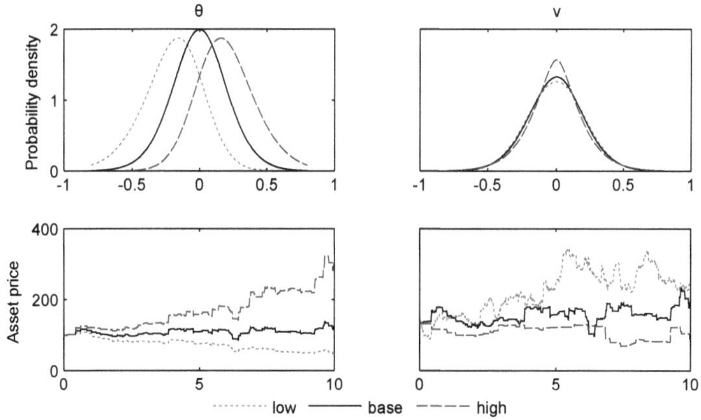

Figure 11: The VG model: Parameter sensitivities. $T = 10$, $S(0) = 100$, $\mu = 0$, $\sigma = 0.15$, $\theta = -0.1, 0, 0.1$, $\nu = 0.05, 0.3, 1$. See footnote of fig. 9 for more details.

the parameter θ gives us control over the skewness and ν influences the peak of the distribution. As expected, we observe rising price paths for positively skewed returns (here, more positive returns occur) and less volatile price path for a highly peaked distribution (fewer extreme events occur).

Another popular and flexible Lévy process is the NIG model. Similarly to the VG process, the model can be expressed as a time-changed Brownian motion, where the time process is governed by an Inverse Gaussian distribution. Letting $S(t)$ denote the price path, then, for time $s \leq t$ and $a, b \in \mathbb{R}$, we can write $S(t) - S(s) \sim \mathcal{IG}(a(t-s,b))$ (Kienitz & Wetterau, 2012). As the SDE representation follows the same logic as under the VG process, we can, therefore, confidently move on to the discrete time representation without any loss of additional insights. The asset price under the historical probability measure at time t is governed by the following expression:

$$S(t) = S(0)\exp\left[\mu t + \beta\delta^2 Y + \delta\sqrt{Y}W(t)\right] \tag{4.1.19}$$

$$Y = \theta + \frac{\theta}{2t^2}\left(\theta z^2 - \sqrt{2\theta t^2 Z + \theta^2 z^2}\right), \quad z \sim \mathcal{N}(0,1)$$

$$\theta = \frac{t}{\delta\sqrt{\alpha^2 - \beta^2}},$$

where α, β, and δ are the NIG specific input parameters. Based on Kienitz and Wetterau (2012) the martingale adjustment is given by

$$\mu = r + \delta\left(\sqrt{\alpha^2 - (\beta+1)^2} - \sqrt{\alpha^2 - \beta^2}\right). \tag{4.1.20}$$

and the return density can be computed explicitly according to

$$f_{NIG}(x) = \frac{\alpha}{\pi}\frac{K_1\left(\alpha\delta t\sqrt{1+\left(\frac{x-\mu t}{\delta t}\right)^2}\right)}{\sqrt{1+\left(\frac{x-\mu t}{\delta t}\right)^2}}\exp\left(\delta t\left(\sqrt{\alpha^2-\beta^2} + \beta\left(\frac{x-\mu t}{\delta t}\right)\right)\right), \tag{4.1.21}$$

where K is, again, the modified Bessel function of the third kind with an index of one.

Next, an overview is given about how the three NIG specific parameters affect the distribution of returns and price paths. The first parameter α determines the variance of the distribution. Low values lead to high volatility and fat tails, which

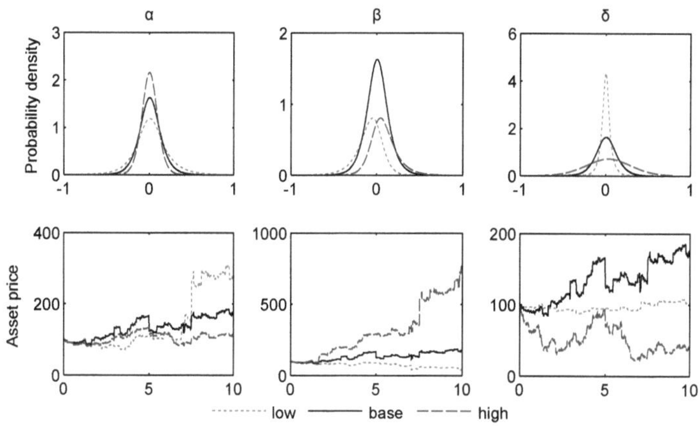

Figure 12: The NIG model: Parameter sensitivities. $T = 10$, $S(0) = 100$, $\mu = 0$, $\alpha = 2, 5, 10$, $\beta = -4, 0.5, 4$, $\delta = 0.05, 0.2, 0.8$. See footnote of fig. 9 for more details.

translate into extreme price movements. β affects all moments of the distribution. In our example, it can be observed that high values for β raise the expectation and skewness while the opposite is true for low betas. The third parameter δ controls the peakedness and variance of the density, such that low parameter values lead to more probability mass in the centre and high values in the tails. The influence on the volatility of price trajectories is clearly observable.

The next and last process that is considered is in analogy to the Bates model, where we were able to summarise the characteristics of jumps and stochastic volatility in one process. Here, we want to augment the NIG (jump) process with stochastic volatility. This is not only consistent with our earlier observation of time-dependent volatility in commodity returns, but also fits the intuitive argument that the environment changes over time so that a static level of uncertainty is difficult to justify (Schoutens, 2003). To introduce stochastic volatility into the NIG process, we employ the logic developed by Carr, Geman, Madan, and Yor (2003), who contend that "random changes in volatility can [...] be captured by random changes in time" (p. 351). In other words, the level of uncertainty can be increased (decreased) by speeding up (slowing down) the rate at which time passes. Without

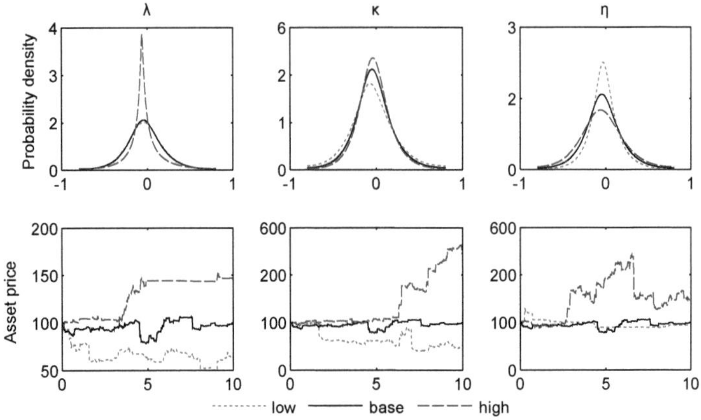

Figure 13: The NIG-CIR model: Parameter sensitivities. $T = 10$, $S(0) = 100$, $\mu = 0$, $\alpha = 5$, $\beta = 0.5$, $\delta = 0.2$, $\lambda = 0.01, 0.5, 3$, $\kappa = 0.005, 1, 3$, $\eta = 0.05, 0.5, 1$. See footnote of fig. 9 for more details.

digressing to much into technicalities, we want to compute

$$S(t) = S(0)\exp\left(\mu t + L(Y(t))\right), \tag{4.1.22}$$

where L is the NIG process and Y is a monotonically increasing and mean-reverting square root CIR process (Carr et al., 2003; Kienitz & Wetterau, 2012), which governs the stochastic evolution of time. Note that it must be monotonically increasing as time cannot go backward. As the analytical solutions to the formula stated above and the return density are somewhat cumbersome, these are not presented here for more convenient reading. However, I provide details on the implementation in Matlab file *path_nigcir* and kindly refer the reader to Carr et al. (2003) and Kienitz and Wetterau (2012) for further reference. Instead, let us directly proceed with the graphical analysis of parameter sensitivities. Please note that since we are already familiar with the parameters α, β, and δ from the standalone NIG process, we limit our attention only to the parameters governing the stochastic time change or volatility.

As we can observe, all of the three parameters influence the kurtosis of the distribution, however, in a different way and with diverse impacts on the price trajectories.

While it is generally in line with expectations that stochastic volatility affects the "fat-taildness" of the distribution, a distinctive interpretation of each parameter is less intuitive. For our purposes, however, it suffices to notice that we gain even more control over the distribution shape at the cost of a additional parameters with similar influence on the distribution so that calibration results could be unstable.

4.2 Model selection

Now that have a range of models at hand, the next step is to assess their relative goodness of fit to past commodity return data. To do so, this section is split into two parts. First, a flexible and effective calibration method is introduced to obtain the optimal parameter sets for each of the previous stochastic processes across the 14 commodities in the sample. Second, given these parameters we check the relative ability of each process to capture the statistical properties of past commodity return data based on an in-sample and out-of-sample test to detect possible *overfitting*.

4.2.1 Calibration

The calibration of *advanced* stochastic processes in our context is in some sense not a trivial task. As the previously discussed models are mostly envisaged for the pricing of market traded options, existing literature propagates the calibration of these processes to a basket of such options with different strike prices and maturities to capture information about the implied volatility surface. In particular, it is common to algorithmically minimise some measure of distance (e.g. the root mean squared error) between option prices in the basket and model prices subject to the input parameters. This procedure directly yields the risk-neutral parametrisation of the process, based upon which the pricing model is build. While the calibration to option prices has the advantage to be forward looking in the sense that prices reflect the aggregated opinion of all market participants on future payoffs, data availability on a basket of commodity options may resemble an obstacle for corporate finance practitioners in non-financial institutions. As a result, I presume that in a real options context it is much more convenient and flexible to be able to back out the parameters from a series of historical commodity prices directly. Along these lines a number of methods have been suggested. Gibson and Schwartz (1990) propose a seemingly unrelated regression model to fit mean-reverting models, Schwartz (1997) and Manoliu and Tompaidis (2002) employ a state space representation to estimate a number of mean-reverting models with the Kalman filter, Brigo et al. (2007) apply MLE for the Merton and VG model, Seneta (2004) uses moment matching to fit the VG process, and Brooks and Prokopczuk (2013) employ the Markov chain Monte Carlo method to fit various stochastic volatility models. While, I am sure, the list can be continued for a while, none of the above methods appears satisfactory for our purposes as they are either not general enough to work for all our processes or require mathematically involved adaptations in each case.

Instead, I propose to minimise an appropriate measure of distance between the kernel density estimate of historical returns and the analytical probability density of the model under appropriate constraints and with a suitable algorithm. The idea is to choose the process parameters in such a way that the model implied return density mimics the empirical return distribution as closely as possible. As suggested, for instance, by Schoutens (2003) or Brigo et al. (2007), this is what characterises a good model fit. For easier reference, I will call the proposed method Algorithmic Probability Density Fitting (APDF) in the remainder of this document. To familiarise the reader with the idea of APDF, we will next consider the choice of an objective function and an appropriate algorithm. Thereafter, the calibration results are benchmarked against MLE estimates and some implementation details are considered.

Plausible objective functions include, for instance, the root mean squared error, the sum of squared errors, the average percentage error, and the sum of absolute errors. Since, however, a measure involving squaring the distance penalises large deviations of the model from the empirical distribution more than many small ones (with equivalent sum of absolute errors), the sum of squared errors fits my desire to replicate the distribution shape as accurately as possible. While it could be considered to add some weight function to put more emphasis on deviations in the distribution tail, I leave such experiments to further study as the choice of a sensible weight function deserves some separate attention. The quantity we want to minimise is given by

$$SSE = \sum_{i=1}^{N} \left(\hat{f}_{Kernel}(i) - f_{Model}(i)\right)^2, \tag{4.2.1}$$

where SSE denotes the sum of squared errors, $\hat{f}_{Kernel}$ is the kernel density estimate of past returns for a given commodity calculated according to (3.2.13), and f_{Model} is the model implied probability density. Where the model density is not explicitly available, it is derived from the characteristic function of the process. The SSE is computed on a grid of $N = 2^{16}$ points, where an exponential of two is chosen to speed up the Fourier transform algorithm when the density is computed from the characteristic function.[44] The grid is chosen such that it encompasses the entire spectrum of historically observed returns. Note that in subsequent analyses of model fit, I will report the Average Squared Error (ASE), which is the SSE divided by the number of grid points N. This simply facilitates the comparison of results in case a different number of grid points is used in the density calculations.

Next, to minimise the objective function there is a choice between direct search methods (Nelder-Mead), Newton based algorithms (Levenberg-Marquardt, L-BFGS, Sequential quadratic programming), and stochastic optimisers (Differential Evolution (DE), Simulated Annealing (SA)), which are globally convergent, i.e. do not get stuck in local minima (Kienitz & Wetterau, 2012). As experiments reveal that local optimisers do not converge to a sensible solution and since computation time is not a highly critical argument in our context, it follows logically to choose among the stochastic optimisers, where the solution is less dependent on the choice

[44] See, for instance, Kienitz and Wetterau (2012).

of initial parameter values and, thereby, gives us somewhat greater flexibility in the application to different models. Further experiments show that DE is even more reliable than SA, albeit lower computation speed. Eventually, I decide to use DE in the form originally proposed by Storn and Price (1995) using the open source *DeMat* toolbox.[45] To further improve calibration results and save computation time, I combine DE with Pattern Search (PS), a direct search Matlab routine for constrained optimisation problems. In other words, once DE has finished computation, the parameter results are passed on to initialise PS for further optimisation. A scheme of this kind is also known as *hybrid optimisation*, meaning that a global optimiser is used first to circumvent local minima in the objective function followed by a faster local optimiser to fine-tune results (Kienitz & Wetterau, 2012). Please note that I use PS instead of other, potentially faster hybrid optimisers as it can cope with discontinuities in the objective function. While a detailed discussion of the algorithms is beyond the scope of this paper, let me say that the logic of DE relies on the principles of inheritance, mutation, recombination, selection, and crossover. Roughly speaking, the algorithm starts out with a an initial population of candidates that are evaluated based on their *fitness* to minimise the objective function. This population is subsequently mutated in a way that the fittest candidates evolve and an optimal value for the objective or fitness function is reached.[46] In order to verify next that the method yields acceptable calibration results, I compare parameter estimates for GBM, the Merton, and VG model under MLE and APDF. The choice of these processes is motivated by the desire to have a range of diverse models, which admit the calibration by a popular alternative calibration method such as MLE for benchmarking. Since the technicalities of MLE calibration are not of primary interest in our context, details are summarised in appendix B. The graphical representation of calibration results shows that both MLE and

[45]The toolbox is available from `http://www1.icsi.berkeley.edu/~storn/code.html`.

[46]In subsequent calculations the initial population is set to 20 or 30, depending on the number of parameters to be estimated, the mutation scaling factor is set to 0.8, the crossover probability is 0.85, and the number of generations is set between 500 and 1000 depending, again, on the number of parameters to be estimated. PS is run with default settings. Note that this set-up is conservative in the sense that also fewer population members and mutation generations should lead to an optimum. For details see Storn and Price (1995).

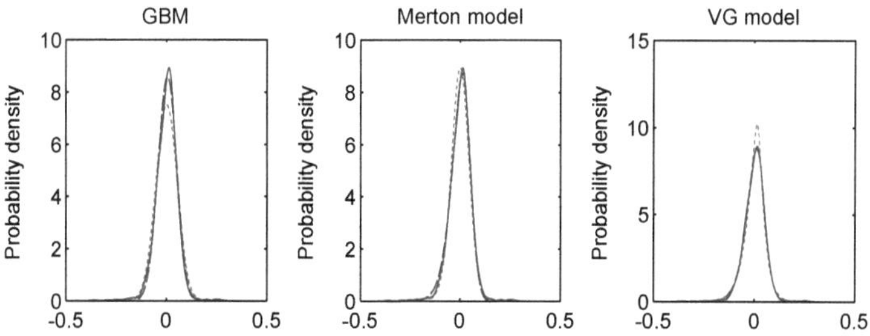

Figure 14: Comparing MLE and APDF. The plots show the empirical kernel density estimate (green) and the analytical return distribution for each model based on MLE parameter estimates (light grey) and APDF (dark grey). Parameter estimates (MLE/APDF) for weekly crude oil log returns over the full sample period (02/08/1993 - 30/12/2013) for GBM: $\mu = 0.0016/0.0056$, $\sigma = 0.0531/0.0464$. Corresponding parameter estimates for the Merton model: $\mu = 0.0016/0.0016, \sigma = 0.0428/0.0366, \mu_J = -0.0291/-0.0565, \sigma_J = 0.1255/0.01, \lambda = 0.0598/0.3271$. Parameter estimates for the VG model: $\mu = 0.016/0.0299, \sigma = 0.0506/0.0481, \theta = -0.0144/-0.0290, \nu = 0.6011/0.2467$. The empirical kernel and analytical (transition) densities are evaluated based on the above stated parameters on a grid of 1000 points.

APDF parameter estimates yield a close fit to the historical return distribution, however, the fit generated by APDF is evidently even closer, especially for the VG process. This insight is quantified in table 6, where we can observe that the ASE between historical and model implied densities is lower if parameters are calibrated with APDF instead of MLE.[47] From these results, we can conclude that APDF can be considered an appropriate technique for empirical parameter estimation in the next subsection.

Before we turn to the goodness of fit results, however, let me outline three minor implementation details necessary to assure that the APDF delivers sensible parameter estimates. First, in the case of the Heston and Bates model, I constrain the long-term variance Θ to equal the initial variance v_0 in order to keep the return density independent of time. If, for instance, the variance process was allowed to decrease to a lower long-term level, the return distribution would become more peaked as time progresses. Since this time dependence cannot be captured by the objective function, calibration results would be potentially unreasonable. Note that

[47] Note that this conclusion does not change if other distance measures such as the sum of absolute errors or average absolute errors are used, which were not minimised in the APDF objective function.

Table 6:
MLE and APDF model fit

For each calibration method and model, the parameter sets described in fig. 14 are used. In the *Analytical* columns, the ASE is calculated between the empirical kernel density estimate and the model density given by its probability density function as in fig. 14. For the *Kernel* columns, 100,000 returns are generated for each model and their kernel density estimate is compared to the empirical one. This comparison is added to double-check the reliability of parameter estimates in Monte Carlo applications.

	GBM		Merton		VG	
	Analytical	Kernel	Analytical	Kernel	PDF	Kernel
MLE	0.142	0.168	0.096	0.068	0.076	0.066
APDF	0.038	0.039	0.013	0.014	0.007	0.007

the necessity of this constraint is a weakness of APDF as a calibration methodology for models exhibiting such time dependence in the return distribution. Second, I impose the *Feller property* on the Heston and Bates model.[48] This ensures that the processes, in particular the variance process, cannot hit zero. Clearly, prices of zero or deterministic prices without uncertainty are not meaningful projections of the future. Third, in the Merton, Bates, and NIG-CIR model, I constrain the drift to equal the historic mean return. For the former two models this is helpful as the algorithm could otherwise compensate an overestimated mean with overestimated negative jumps. Controlling the location of the distribution eliminates this potential problem and improves convergence, particularly in the NIG-CIR model. While this kind of instability issue can always occur if two or more parameters control the distribution shape in a similar way, this is an unavoidable evil in the other cases and needs to be controlled via plausibility checks.

4.2.2 Goodness of fit

In this subsection, it is discussed which model is likely to yield the best fit to historical commodity returns. To do so, we will draw on the previously developed logic and compare the ASE between the empirical distribution estimate and the model implied distribution with APDF-fitted parameters. Since complex models with many parameters such as the Bates or NIG-CIR process generally outper-

[48] According to Kienitz and Wetterau (2012) the condition holds if $2\kappa\Theta \geq \nu^2$.

form simpler models in in-sample tests, but not in out-of-sample tests (Bakshi, Cao, & Zhiwu, 1997), two different test set-ups are created. First, an in-sample test, where the ASE is calculated with historical density and parameter estimates based on the full sample period from 1993 to 2013. Second, an out-of-sample test, where model parameters are calibrated over the period 1993 - 2004 and the resulting model distribution is compared to the empirical density of the period 1995 - 2013. Clearly, the choice of calibration and analysis period in the out-of-sample test is drastic as several *extreme* events occurred during the analysis period (ascent of prices after 2005 and financial crisis), which are very different from events observed during the calibration period. An additional way of out-of-sample testing could involve a leave-one-out cross validation as suggested by De Laurentis et al. (2010), however, this exercise is left to further study as the main purpose is equally well accomplished by the here adopted simple alternative. This is to understand if the nuances in the shape of return distributions that more complex models are able to capture persist over time so that it is worthwhile to account for them. In order to conserve space, I report the calibrated process parameters after some sanity checks in appendix A4.

The results, shown in table 7, can be analysed in a number of ways. Considering first the in-sample results (setting one), we may notice that GBM leads to the worst fit in all cases and the Bates model to the best in most cases. Only for nickel, zinc, and silver the VG process fits better to past data and in the case of corn, the NIG model ranks best. When judged by the mean ASE (in brackets) across commodities, we have the following rank order from best fit to worst: Bates (0.0059), VG (0.0104), NIG (0.0108), NIG-CIR (0.0156), Merton (0.0260), Heston (0.0270), GBM (0.0962). As the Bates model is with nine parameters in some sense the most flexible one, the results are generally little surprising. However, I would have expected the NIG-CIR process to have a better fit than the stand-alone NIG process. However, while this expectation is not confirmed on average, it is fulfilled in the cases of oil and cocoa. When analysing the results by commodity, it is evident

Table 7:

Average squared fitting errors

For each resource and stochastic process, the ASE is reported for two different settings. Setting one refers to the in-sample test, where parameters are calibrated and model fit is analysed over the same period: 02/08/1993 - 30/12/2013. Setting two is the out-of-sample test with calibration period 02/08/1993 - 27/12/2004 and analysis of fit during 03/01/2005 - 30/12/2013. The parameter estimates corresponding to this table are obtained from APDF and are reported in appendix A4 and A5.

		Average squared fitting errors						
Resource	Setting	GBM	Heston	Merton	Bates	VG	NIG	NIG-CIR
Oil	1	0.038	0.008	0.013	0.006	0.007	0.009	0.007
	2	0.054	0.025	0.030	0.025	0.024	0.026	0.024
Aluminum	1	0.143	0.043	0.054	0.012	0.021	0.028	0.039
	2	0.499	0.382	0.453	0.365	0.365	0.373	0.376
Copper	1	0.075	0.029	0.035	0.008	0.012	0.012	0.028
	2	0.255	0.221	0.213	0.195	0.202	0.201	0.191
Lead	1	0.144	0.051	0.063	0.005	0.016	0.020	0.032
	2	0.756	0.627	0.650	0.570	0.575	0.583	0.590
Nickel	1	0.044	0.006	0.008	0.002	0.002	0.002	0.003
	2	0.121	0.080	0.084	0.080	0.075	0.075	0.076
Zinc	1	0.093	0.024	0.026	0.010	0.008	0.010	0.016
	2	0.992	0.892	0.886	0.868	0.856	0.862	0.867
Gold	1	0.349	0.087	0.066	0.011	0.039	0.024	0.033
	2	2.023	1.639	1.534	1.485	1.569	1.544	1.522
Silver	1	0.078	0.024	0.024	0.005	0.005	0.005	0.012
	2	0.366	0.292	0.280	0.259	0.264	0.263	0.269
Wheat	1	0.044	0.027	0.008	0.005	0.008	0.006	0.008
	2	0.273	0.230	0.229	0.227	0.228	0.225	0.230
Corn	1	0.087	0.019	0.013	0.004	0.003	0.003	0.007
	2	0.269	0.196	0.174	0.173	0.176	0.175	0.181
Soybeans	1	0.073	0.017	0.017	0.006	0.007	0.006	0.013
	2	0.189	0.120	0.106	0.104	0.110	0.112	0.114
Sugar	1	0.031	0.006	0.006	0.004	0.005	0.004	0.006
	2	0.032	0.011	0.022	0.008	0.009	0.008	0.012
Coffee	1	0.020	0.006	0.006	0.001	0.003	0.003	0.006
	2	0.123	0.099	0.101	0.095	0.099	0.098	0.099
Cocoa	1	0.127	0.032	0.026	0.007	0.010	0.020	0.010
	2	0.246	0.133	0.115	0.108	0.114	0.131	0.109

that gold has the highest mean ASE (0.087) and coffee the lowest (0.006), indicating that processes have on average the greatest difficulties to mimic the shape of the gold return distribution while it works best for coffee.

Turning to the out-of-sample setting, we may notice that the fit generally worsens. While the mean model ASE per mean commodity is 0.027 in setting one, it rises to 0.353 in setting two. The extent to which model fit worsens depends, however, on the commodity we consider. For instance, the mean ASE for sugar rises only relatively little from 0.009 to 0.015, which is in sharp contrast to the case of gold, where the mean ASE jumps from 0.087 to 1.617. This can be explained by the changing gold price dynamics, which exhibit an almost steadily increasing level of volatility over time (see appendix A2). Although, this was not enough to reject stationarity of gold returns previously (see table 4), even this change of return distribution between calibration and analysis period suffices to worsen model fit considerably. With respect to the rank order of models, it is somewhat surprising and almost in contrast to the argument that processes with many parameters are easily *overfitted*[49] that the Bates model retains the best average fit also in the out-of-sample test. However, the relative advantage over the second best process shrinks.[50] Also, the Bates model delivers only the best model fit for 50 per cent of the commodities compared to 71 per cent in setting one. For the purpose of completeness, we have the following rank order in setting two: Bates (0.3258), NIG-CIR (0.3329), VG (0.3334), NIG (0.3340), Merton (0.3483), Heston (0.3534), GBM (0.4428). Please note that these figures are, again, average ASEs over all commodities for each model.

In summary, the analysis shows that in both test settings advanced stochastic processes with more parameters relative to GBM lead to considerably lower fitting errors. While it is not uniformly clear across commodities which model is the most favourable one, particularly the Bates, VG, and NIG process appear gener-

[49] See, for instance, Bakshi et al. (1997).

[50] In setting one, the mean ASE is 42.6% lower for the Bates model than the second best VG process. This advantages shrinks to 2.1% vis-á-vis the second best NIG-CIR process in setting two, the out-of-sample test.

ally good choices. Accounting furthermore for potential difficulties in calibrating the high number of parameters in the Bates model, the VG or NIG model resemble almost equally powerful and easy to handle alternatives.

5 Capital budgeting implications

Having identified considerable differences in the ability of stochastic processes to replicate the properties of historical price series, we do not yet know to what extent process choice also influences the valuation of capital investments. While Lo and Wang (1995) show that the choice between GBM and a mean-reverting Ornstein-Uhlenbeck process can affect financial call option values in the order of 5%, Tsekrekos et al. (2012) identify much larger variations in a more complex real option investment ranging between -40 % and 25%. However, their analysis is entirely based on comparisons between the classical mean-reverting commodity price processes of Schwartz (1997) so that an analysis of valuation implications based on the different perspective advocated in this paper is yet unavailable in academic literature. As a result, two questions need to be answered in this section. First, does the choice among previously discussed stochastic processes influence the valuation result of commodity-linked contingent claims? Second, if valuation differences arise, are these equally pronounced across investments with different degrees of flexibility or maturities? The latter of the two questions follows from the diverse findings of Lo and Wang (1995) and Tsekrekos et al. (2012), which implicitly suggest that stochastic process choice matters more in complex real option applications than in the context of financial options.

5.1 A stylised investment project

In order to answer the previously formulated questions, a stylised capital investment project with different levels of flexibility is considered. The set-up of this project is motivated by the desire to expose the influence of stochastic process choice on capital budgeting decisions from a range of different angles. In this highly stylised example, a natural resource company has the opportunity to bid on the extraction rights for ore bauxite, the basis for aluminium production. Under the agreement, the firm is entitled to start production whenever desired and it is estimated that once started, it will take five years to exploit the deposit. The required production site at the mine can be set up with negligible time delay after the investment decision has been made. Now, to turn this setting into a highly stylised valuation case study, the project value will be given as a combination of a static NPV, an option to defer investment for five years (decision period), and the option to abandon the site for a salvage value (net of administrative accompaniment) once production has been started (operating period). For simplicity, it is assumed that the operating period is limited to five years. Alternatively, one could fix the total quantity of ore bauxite in the mine and let the project last until the resource is fully depleted (Brennan & Schwartz, 1985). All inputs and corresponding notation related to the investment project are summarised in appendix A6.

In order to flexibly implement the valuation for different stochastic processes, I use the Least Squares Monte Carlo (LSM) technique proposed by Longstaff and Schwartz (2001) to estimate continuation values and optimal stopping rules in the valuation. This is in line with Gamba (2003) and Tsekrekos et al. (2012), who show that LSM can be successfully applied not only to American financial options, but also to potentially more complex capital investment projects. On this basis, I compute three quantities. First, the *static* project NPV based on the risk-neutral expectation of future aluminium prices if the project is started immediately. Second, the NPV with the flexibility to abandon the project for a salvage value within the five operating years but, again, assuming an immediate project start. Third, the option value to defer investment for up to five years. From these quantities, the separate option values and the total project value including all flexibility can be calculated.

To begin with, the project's operating cash flow at time t based on stochastic process m and commodity price path ω is given by

$$CF_o\left(t, S_m(t,\omega)\right) = qr \cdot \left(S_m(t,\omega) - c\right) - K - \text{Tax} \tag{5.1.1}$$

$$\text{Tax} = \left[\tau\left(qr \cdot \left(S_m(t,\omega) - c\right) - K\right), 0\right]^+ .$$

Please note that superscript + denotes the maximum of a set of values. The cash flow calculation is similar to the one used in the classical natural resource investment example by Brennan and Schwartz (1985), however, I omit several details such as the adjustment of costs to inflation to avoid any unnecessary complexity that distracts from the main idea of this section. Next, I calculate the gross project value (gross of the initial investment) for each possible starting date with and without incorporating the possibility to abandon the project for a salvage value (η). As future commodity prices are uncertain and not part of the investor's information set, the LSM method is used in the backward recursion to estimate the expected project value in the subsequent period. Beginning in the last of the five operating years T_j of the project when started in year j, where $0 \leq j \leq 5$, the project value in T_j is given by

$$PV\left(T_j, S_m\left(T_j, \omega\right)\right) = \left[CF_o\left(T_j, S_m\left(T_j, \omega\right)\right), \eta\right]^+, \tag{5.1.2}$$

i.e. the maximum of the operating cash flow in the last period and the salvage value received upon abandonment.[51] Now, for $t_j = T_j - 1, \ldots, 0$, the project value in time t is given recursively by

$$PV\left(t_j, S_m\left(t_j, \omega\right)\right) = \left\{CF_o\left(t_j, S_m\left(t_j, \omega\right)\right) + \Phi\left(t_j, S_m\left(t_j, \omega\right)\right), \eta\right\}^+, \tag{5.1.3}$$

where Φ denotes the expected project value in the subsequent period under the risk-neutral, equivalent probability measure $\mathbb{Q}$. More formally, this quantity can be written as

$$\Phi\left(t_j, S_m\left(t_j, \omega\right)\right) = \mathbb{E}_{t_j}^{\mathbb{Q}}\left[\sum_{t_i = t_j + 1}^{T_j} e^{-r(t_i - t_j)} CF_o\left(t_i, S_m\left(t_i, \omega\right)\right)\right]. \tag{5.1.4}$$

In other words, the project value in each period is either the sum of the operating cash flow received in that period and the sum of expected discounted future cash

[51]Alternatively, one could have modelled the salvage value in direct proportion to the remaining quantity of ore bauxite in the mine, however, this introduces some unnecessary complexity to the problem.

flows until maturity if operation is optimal. Or, if operation is not optimal, the project value in period t is simply the salvage value as no future cash inflows can be expected once the project is abandoned. To account for the possibility of different starting dates due to the option to wait, subscript j was introduced to indicate the respective starting time of the rolling five-year operating horizon. More specifically, if the project is started in year three, the corresponding present value in period three is calculated with $j=3$ and $T_j=8$, following from the five-year operating horizon. However, as stated previously, future aluminium prices are uncertain so that (5.1.4) cannot be readily calculated at a given time step (Gamba, 2003). Instead, the continuation value Φ is embedded in the project value step-by-step during the backward recursion according to

$$\begin{aligned} PV\left(t_j, S_m\left(t_j, \omega\right)\right) = \{ & CF_o\left(t_j, S_m\left(t_j, \omega\right)\right) \\ & + e^{-r\Delta t}\mathbb{E}_{t_j}^{\mathbb{Q}}\left[PV\left(t_j+1, S_m\left(t_j+1, \omega\right)\right)\right], \eta\}^{+}. \end{aligned} \tag{5.1.5}$$

This is often referred to as the Bellman equation (Tsekrekos et al., 2012), which does not involve all future operating dates t_i to calculate Φ as would (5.1.4), but only relies on the project value one step ahead. This is estimated according to the LSM method by first regressing the project's discounted value of the subsequent period onto an appropriate basis $\{L_n(t, CF_o(t,S))\}$ and subsequently using the obtained regression coefficients to project the expected continuation value as a function of current operating cash flows evaluated through the set of basis functions. Omitting some of the previous notation for convenience, we can express Φ as

$$e^{-r\Delta t}\mathbb{E}_t^{\mathbb{Q}}\left[PV(t+1)\,|CF_o(t)\right] = \sum_{n=1}^{N} \phi_n(t) L_n(CF_o(t,S)) + \varepsilon, \tag{5.1.6}$$

where ϕ is the set of regression coefficients corresponding to the value of each basis function through which the project cash flow at a given time and commodity path is evaluated. The set of coefficients is chosen such that the residual term

ε is minimised in a least squares sense (Kienitz & Wetterau, 2012). Given the coefficients, the continuation value of a project at time t is given in sparse notation by

$$\hat{\Phi}(t, CF_o(t,S)) = \hat{\phi}_1 L_1(t, CF_o(t,S)) +, \ldots, + \hat{\phi}_N L_N(t, CF_o(t,S)), \tag{5.1.7}$$

where the first six terms of the family of weighted Laguerre polynomials, denoted by L, are used as basis functions (see appendix B5).[52]

Once the backward recursion is completed for each starting date in the decision horizon for the case with and without abandonment flexibility ((5.1.2) and (5.1.5) are modified accordingly), I obtain two grids of gross project values with dimensions equal to the number of paths and time steps in the decision horizon. Taking the average of project values across all paths in $t = 0$ and subtracting the initial investment, I obtain the corresponding NPV with and without abandonment flexibility when the project is started immediately. As a last step, the additional value arising from the possibility to defer investment can be calculated as a call option on the gross project value with maturity equal to the length of the decision horizon and a strike price equal to the investment cost adjusted for the time value of money (Trigeorgis, 1996). Thus, the value of the option to defer (for each commodity price path ω) is given by

$$\begin{aligned} V(T,\omega) &= \left[PV(T,\omega) - Ie^{rT}, 0\right]^{+} \\ V(t,\omega) &= \left[PV(t,\omega) - Ie^{rt}, V(t+1,\omega)\right]^{+}, \quad t = T-1,\ldots,0. \end{aligned} \tag{5.1.8}$$

As outlined above, the continuation value, denoted by $V(t+1,\omega)$, is estimated recursively with the LSM method.[53] The option value to wait is finally computed as the average across all paths V in time zero.

[52] See Abramowitz and Stegun (1964) for further reference. Please note also that the choice of other eligible orthogonal basis functions such as Hermite or Chebyshev polynomials converge to similar results if enough terms are included (Tsekrekos et al., 2012). As a result, no further experiments are conducted in this direction.

[53] Note that contrary to Gamba (2003) or Tsekrekos et al. (2012), I use only so-called *in-the-money* paths in the estimation of regression coefficients as this improves convergence of results (Longstaff & Schwartz, 2001).

Before turning to the valuation results, let me kindly refer you also to the complementary Excel spreadsheet where a fully worked out example is provided for a more lively illustration of this investment project.

5.2 Results

The results presented in table 8 indicate that the choice of stochastic processes has a considerable effect on project valuation. It stands out that the use of GBM leads to the lowest valuation estimates throughout. On average, GBM undervalues the project by 14.3% relative to the empirically more appropriate alternative processes. One explanation for this finding may result from the classical idea that higher uncertainty creates value when payoff structures are asymmetric. In other words, when volatility is high, an option holder benefits from more frequent extreme movements as he can gain when prices evolve in his favour, but has a limited downside when the opposite is true (Hull, 2009). As all processes except GBM can account for the empirically observed fat-tails, i.e. a higher probability of extreme events than presumed under GBM, it is plausible that project values should be higher using such processes. This logic is consistent with the observation that valuations are highest under the Bates and NIG-CIR process, which imply the combined uncertainty arising from jumps and stochastic volatility.

In order to ascertain that the previously presented results cannot be explained by sampling error, I use the same pseudo random number stream in each valuation[54] and provide upper and lower bounds for the valuation estimates at the 95% confidence level in panel A of fig. 15.

Besides the impact of different processes on valuation results, it is of practical relevance to investigate how optimal investment behaviour depends on the stochastic price model. To this end, I depict the critical aluminium price as a function of time, above which management should proceed with investment.[55] As we would expect,

[54]Please note that valuation results do not change subject to the choice of a different random number stream.

[55]In mathematical finance, this critical price is often referred to as the *free boundary* that separates early exercise from continuation region in American-style derivatives (Battauz & Ortu, 2009).

Table 8:

Capital investment project: Valuation results

The parameters underlying the valuation results are reported in appendix A4 and A6. NPV_0 denotes the static project net present value without any flexibility. *O2A* refers to the option value from abandonment. NPV_1 resembles the project NPV including this abandonment flexibility. *O2W* denotes the option value to wait. NPV_2 is the project value including both the flexibility to abandon and to wait. *CRR* refers to the valuation results obtained from the binomial lattice of Cox et al. (1979) with parametrisation corresponding to GBM in the Monte Carlo simulation. The *CRR* valuation is added as a reference point and to confirm the reliability of the LSM algorithm in this setting. Please note that all valuations are performed using the same global pseudo random number stream for better comparability. Results are reported in US$ '000s.

		CCR	GBM	Heston	Merton	Bates	VG	NIG	NIG-CIR
	NPV_0	-256.92	-256.95	-266.37	-266.08	-266.64	-268.33	-269.37	-268.30
+	O2A	294.60	293.40	316.72	317.59	326.23	320.55	324.11	324.37
=	NPV_1	37.68	36.45	50.35	51.50	59.58	52.23	54.74	56.07
+	O2W	365.29	368.55	398.65	400.98	428.15	403.96	408.85	412.70
=	NPV_2	402.96	405.00	449.00	452.48	487.73	456.19	463.60	468.77

this threshold is declining in time for all processes. Since the decision to invest at each step resembles a comparison between the expected value of waiting and immediate investment and since the value of waiting declines as we move closer to the end of the decision horizon, already a lower commodity price (and corresponding operating cash flow) is sufficient for immediate investment to be optimal. In our context, one may observe in panel B of fig. 15 that critical prices are relatively aligned, but slightly higher for GBM than the remaining models. This suggests that GBM may not only undervalue the project but also lead to overly conservative investment decisions relative to the value maximising policy implied by empirically more appropriate processes.

The flipside of this consideration is the probability of investment as a function of time. Similarly to Schwartz (2004), I compute this quantity as the percentage of paths, for which investment is optimal at each point in time (without conditioning on prior exercise). In line with previous arguments, it is evident from panel C of fig. 15 that under GBM, management would often defer the project start more than optimal.

While the previous paragraphs have already confirmed the importance of stochastic process choice, it is yet unclear whether this conclusion is equally valid for diverse

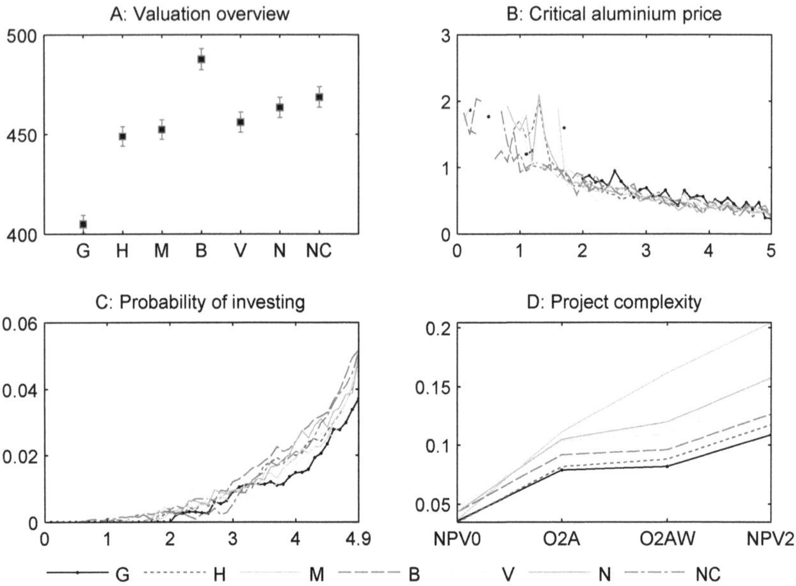

Figure 15: Capital investment project: Valuation analysis. G: GBM, H: Heston, M: Merton, B: Bates, V: VG, N: NIG, NC: NIG-CIR. Panel A depicts the project valuation in US$ '000s including the flexibility to defer and to abandon. Also shown are valuation confidence bounds (95% level). Panel B shows the critical aluminium price in US$ '000s, above which it is optimal to invest and below to wait. This is plotted for the 5 year decision horizon. Panel C illustrates the fraction of paths for which investment is optimal. In the last step of the decision horizon (not shown for more convenient viewing), investment is optimal in 55% of cases with little variation across processes. Panel D depicts the percentage deviation of the value of different project components for all processes relative to GBM. Here, NPV_0 is the static NPV, *O2A* refers to the option to abandon, *O2AW* is the value of the option to wait on the project, which can be abandoned, and NPV_2 is the project NPV including all flexibility.

projects with different degrees of complexity or flexibility. To answer this second question in more detail, panel D of fig. 15 provides the percentage difference of project value for all stochastic processes relative to GBM when different degrees of project flexibility are considered. The idea is that if complexity exacerbates the impact of process choice on valuation results, percentage differences in project value should gradually increase for different processes when more optionality is present in the project. Indeed, it is evident that valuation estimates are relatively similar when only the uncertain, static NPV is estimated, however, as more optionality is added, estimates diverge. This suggests that an appropriate commodity price model is essential for valuation accuracy in complex investment decisions, however, it may even be negligible in simple cases. To confirm this logic, I also compute the price of a simple at-the-money call option on one ton of aluminium with corresponding five-year maturity and observe that all estimated prices differ only in the order of three to eight per cent, i.e. much less than in the previous case where payoffs were more complex.

To sum up, these findings are generally in line with earlier studies of Lo and Wang (1995), Casassus and Collin-Dufresne (2005), Tsekrekos et al. (2012), and Brooks and Prokopczuk (2013), who similarly indicate the relevance of stochastic process choice in the valuation of financial and real assets. While the magnitude of valuation differences ranges between -40% and 30% across studies, it has become clear that this can be explained by diverse levels of uncertainty and flexibility, as well as the length of investment horizons and the underlying commodity.

6 Conclusion

This thesis aimed at providing practically relevant recommendations for the choice of stochastic commodity price models in capital investment valuation. The analysis of empirical price dynamics across a basket of 14 commodities led to the conclusion that popular mean-reverting processes and GBM are in several respects inconsistent with empirical data. In turn, the merits of alternative models known from financial options pricing were analysed in the application to commodity markets. In this context, a practical and flexible calibration scheme was proposed that allowed me to assess the relative goodness of fit of each process to a range of commodities. It was found that all *new* models deliver a considerably better fit to historical commodity price data than GBM. Among the tested models, the best fit is on average achieved by the Bates and VG process, however, accounting for the unfavourably high number of parameters in the Bates model, the VG process resembles a sensible compromise between accuracy and complexity. To gauge the extent to which the choice among different stochastic processes deserves careful attention in practice, a stylised investment project was introduced. The analysis revealed that in this example stochastic process choice may affect project values in the order of 20%. Moreover, it was found that GBM may not only underestimate project value, but also lead to excessive investment deferral under the optimal decision rule relative to empirically more appropriate processes such as the VG model. While the valuation example was exclusively based on aluminium price dynamics, it can be expected that empirically more skewed or fat-tailed commodities such as soybeans or coffee lead to even higher deviations from GBM-based estimates.

These findings may complement existing literature in three main aspects. First, they are based on a relatively broad dataset and bottom-up statistical approach to stochastic process selection with practical recommendations. Second, this study is, to my knowledge, the first to introduce Lévy processes to the world of real options. Third, stochastic models are not considered in isolation, but comprehensively evaluated in their impact on investment valuation and optimal managerial decision making.

However, several topics follow from these insights for future study. In particular, the universe of stochastic processes considered here is only a small subset of modelling possibilities and can be regarded merely as an entry point for future discussion. For instance, the role of stochastic interest rates outlined by Schulmerich (2010) or seasonal price components as mentioned by Brooks and Prokopczuk (2013) have not even been touched upon. Furthermore, the considerations of this thesis could be extended from a single source of uncertainty to the joint distribution of several risk factors that determine investment valuation and optimal decision making. With respect to the proposed APDF calibration scheme, it may be useful to assess to what extent the more forward looking calibration to financial option prices affects parameter estimates and valuation results. Finally, the LSM implementation can be refined by computing regression coefficients and project values based on different random number streams to eliminate a potentially biased valuation estimate (Kienitz & Wetterau, 2012) and antithetic or control variates could be applied to reduce Monte Carlo variance in the study of stochastic processes (Battauz & Ortu, 2009; Tsekrekos et al., 2012).

While this list can be continued in several directions, the overriding principle in future research should mainly reside in the practical application of real options theory to support managerial decision making in an increasingly uncertain environment.

Appendix

Appendix A

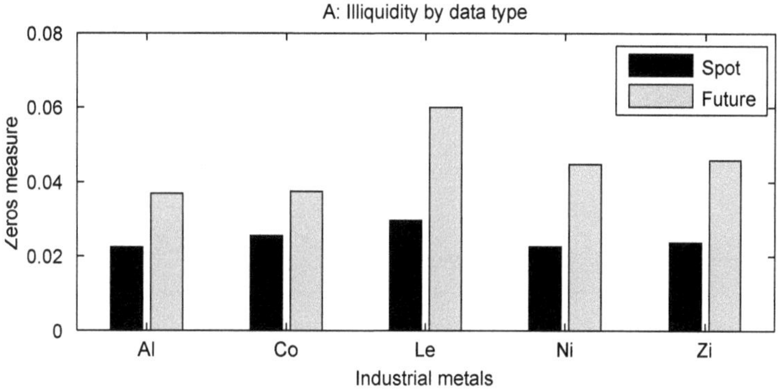

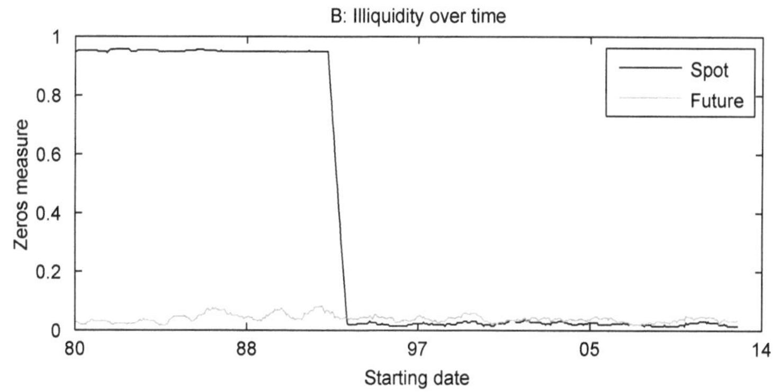

A1: Liquidity of commodity prices. Al: Aluminium, Co: Copper, Le: Lead, NI: Nickel, Zi: Zinc. Panel A shows the *Zeros* metric for daily spot and 3-months future prices from the LME for the period 02/08/1993 - 30/12/2013. Panel B illustrates the development of *Zeros* for daily spot and 3-months future prices for aluminium only. The x-axis denotes the respective starting date for one-year revolving evaluation periods. For convenient viewing only 100 data points are plotted. Note that all non-trading dates have been cleared from the data prior to the analysis.

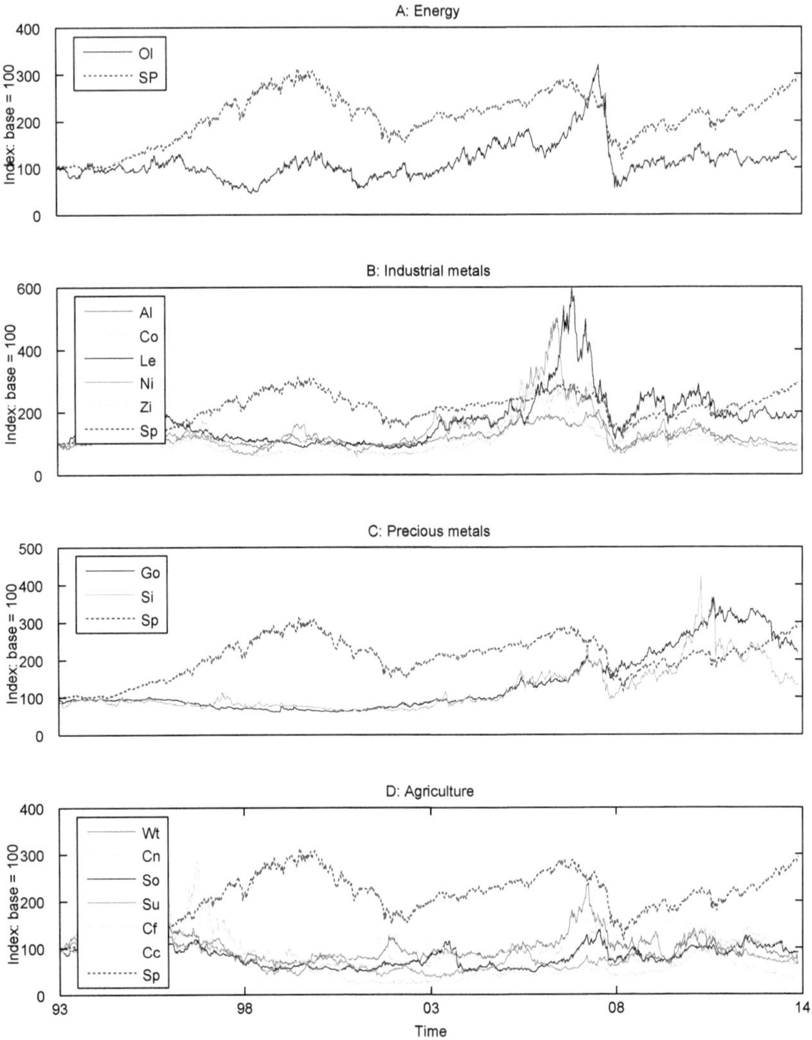

A2: Historical price evolution. Al: Aluminium, Cc: Cocoa, Cf: Coffee, Cn: Corn, Co: Copper, Go: Gold, Le: Lead, Ni: Nickel, Ol: Crude oil, Si: Silver, So: Soybeans, Sp: S&P 500, Su: Sugar, Wt: Wheat, Zi: Zinc. All data is presented for the full sample period: 02/08/1993 - 30/12/2013.

A3: Non-trading dates excluded from dataset (1)

Sources: http://www.londonstockexchange.com/about-the-exchange/company-overview/business-days/business-days.htm, http://www.maa.mhn.de/StarDate/publ_holidays.html.

Year	Ash Wed.	Good Fri.	Easter	Ascension D.	Whitsunday	Christ. E.	Christ. D.	Boxing D.	New Years E.	New Years D.
1980	20/02/1980	04/04/1980	06/04/1980	15/05/1980	25/05/1980	24/12/1980	25/12/1980	26/12/1980	31/12/1980	01/01/1980
1981	04/03/1981	17/04/1981	19/04/1981	28/05/1981	07/06/1981	24/12/1981	25/12/1981	26/12/1981	31/12/1981	01/01/1981
1982	24/02/1982	09/04/1982	11/04/1982	20/05/1982	30/05/1982	24/12/1982	25/12/1982	26/12/1982	31/12/1982	01/01/1982
1983	16/02/1983	01/04/1983	03/04/1983	12/05/1983	22/05/1983	24/12/1983	25/12/1983	26/12/1983	31/12/1983	01/01/1983
1984	07/03/1984	20/04/1984	22/04/1984	31/05/1984	10/06/1984	24/12/1984	25/12/1984	26/12/1984	31/12/1984	01/01/1984
1985	20/02/1985	05/04/1985	07/04/1985	16/05/1985	26/05/1985	24/12/1985	25/12/1985	26/12/1985	31/12/1985	01/01/1985
1986	12/02/1986	28/03/1986	30/03/1986	08/05/1986	18/05/1986	24/12/1986	25/12/1986	26/12/1986	31/12/1986	01/01/1986
1987	04/03/1987	17/04/1987	19/04/1987	28/05/1987	07/06/1987	24/12/1987	25/12/1987	26/12/1987	31/12/1987	01/01/1987
1988	17/02/1988	01/04/1988	03/04/1988	12/05/1988	22/05/1988	24/12/1988	25/12/1988	26/12/1988	31/12/1988	01/01/1988
1989	08/02/1989	24/03/1989	26/03/1989	04/05/1989	14/05/1989	24/12/1989	25/12/1989	26/12/1989	31/12/1989	01/01/1989
1990	28/02/1990	13/04/1990	15/04/1990	24/05/1990	03/06/1990	24/12/1990	25/12/1990	26/12/1990	31/12/1990	01/01/1990
1991	13/02/1991	29/03/1991	31/03/1991	09/05/1991	19/05/1991	24/12/1991	25/12/1991	26/12/1991	31/12/1991	01/01/1991
1992	04/03/1992	17/04/1992	19/04/1992	28/05/1992	07/06/1992	24/12/1992	25/12/1992	26/12/1992	31/12/1992	01/01/1992
1993	24/02/1993	09/04/1993	11/04/1993	20/05/1993	30/05/1993	24/12/1993	25/12/1993	26/12/1993	31/12/1993	01/01/1993
1994	16/02/1994	01/04/1994	03/04/1994	12/05/1994	22/05/1994	24/12/1994	25/12/1994	26/12/1994	31/12/1994	01/01/1994
1995	01/03/1995	14/04/1995	16/04/1995	25/05/1995	04/06/1995	24/12/1995	25/12/1995	26/12/1995	31/12/1995	01/01/1995
1996	21/02/1996	05/04/1996	07/04/1996	16/05/1996	26/05/1996	24/12/1996	25/12/1996	26/12/1996	31/12/1996	01/01/1996
1997	12/02/1997	28/03/1997	30/03/1997	08/05/1997	18/05/1997	24/12/1997	25/12/1997	26/12/1997	31/12/1997	01/01/1997
1998	25/02/1998	10/04/1998	12/04/1998	21/05/1998	31/05/1998	24/12/1998	25/12/1998	26/12/1998	31/12/1998	01/01/1998
1999	17/02/1999	02/04/1999	04/04/1999	13/05/1999	23/05/1999	24/12/1999	25/12/1999	26/12/1999	31/12/1999	01/01/1999
2000	08/03/2000	21/04/2000	23/04/2000	01/06/2000	11/06/2000	24/12/2000	25/12/2000	26/12/2000	31/12/2000	01/01/2000
2001	28/02/2001	13/04/2001	15/04/2001	24/05/2001	03/06/2001	24/12/2001	25/12/2001	26/12/2001	31/12/2001	01/01/2001
2002	13/02/2002	29/03/2002	31/03/2002	09/05/2002	19/05/2002	24/12/2002	25/12/2002	26/12/2002	31/12/2002	01/01/2002
2003	05/03/2003	18/04/2003	20/04/2003	29/05/2003	08/06/2003	24/12/2003	25/12/2003	26/12/2003	31/12/2003	01/01/2003
2004	25/02/2004	09/04/2004	11/04/2004	20/05/2004	30/05/2004	24/12/2004	25/12/2004	26/12/2004	31/12/2004	01/01/2004
2005	09/02/2005	25/03/2005	27/03/2005	05/05/2005	15/05/2005	24/12/2005	25/12/2005	26/12/2005	31/12/2005	01/01/2005

A3: Non-trading dates excluded from dataset (2)

Sources: `http://www.londonstockexchange.com/about-the-exchange/company-overview/business-days/business-days.htm`, `http://www.maa.mhn.de/StarDate/publ_holidays.html`.

Year	Ash Wed.	Good Fri.	Easter	Ascension D.	Whitsunday	Christ. E.	Christ. D.	Boxing D.	New Years E.	New Years D.
2006	01/03/2006	14/04/2006	16/04/2006	25/05/2006	04/06/2006	24/12/2006	25/12/2006	26/12/2006	31/12/2006	01/01/2006
2007	21/02/2007	06/04/2007	08/04/2007	17/05/2007	27/05/2007	24/12/2007	25/12/2007	26/12/2007	31/12/2007	01/01/2007
2008	06/02/2008	21/03/2008	23/03/2008	01/05/2008	11/05/2008	24/12/2008	25/12/2008	26/12/2008	31/12/2008	01/01/2008
2009	25/02/2009	10/04/2009	12/04/2009	21/05/2009	31/05/2009	24/12/2009	25/12/2009	26/12/2009	31/12/2009	01/01/2009
2010	17/02/2010	02/04/2010	04/04/2010	13/05/2010	23/05/2010	24/12/2010	25/12/2010	26/12/2010	31/12/2010	01/01/2010
2011	09/03/2011	22/04/2011	24/04/2011	02/06/2011	12/06/2011	24/12/2011	25/12/2011	26/12/2011	31/12/2011	01/01/2011
2012	22/02/2012	06/04/2012	08/04/2012	17/05/2012	27/05/2012	24/12/2012	25/12/2012	26/12/2012	31/12/2012	01/01/2012
2013	13/02/2013	29/03/2013	31/03/2013	09/05/2013	19/05/2013	24/12/2013	25/12/2013	26/12/2013	31/12/2013	01/01/2013

A4: In-sample APDF: Calibrated parameters (1)

Al: Aluminium, Cc: Cocoa, Cf: Coffee, Cn: Corn, Co: Copper, Go: Gold, Le: Lead, Ni: Nickel, Ol: Crude oil, Si: Silver, So: Soybeans, Su: Sugar, Wt: Wheat, Zi: Zinc. Calibration period: 02/08/1993 - 30/12/2013. Data frequency: Weekly.

		Ol	Al	Co	Le	Ni	Zi	Go	Si	Wt	Cn	So	Su	Cf	Cc
GBM	μ	0.0056	-0.0001	0.0026	0.0014	0.0007	0.0016	0.0016	0.0024	-0.0014	0.0020	0.0017	0.0016	-0.0010	0.0008
	σ	0.0464	0.0272	0.0319	0.0383	0.0445	0.0336	0.0194	0.0349	0.0372	0.0380	0.0318	0.0399	0.0476	0.0337
Heston	μ	0.0016	0.0004	0.0013	0.0017	0.0010	0.0008	0.0010	0.0012	0.0005	0.0006	0.0006	0.0006	0.0005	0.0009
	v_0	0.0025	0.0009	0.0013	0.0018	0.0024	0.0014	0.0005	0.0015	0.0013	0.0018	0.0012	0.0019	0.0027	0.0014
	Θ	0.0025	0.0009	0.0013	0.0018	0.0024	0.0014	0.0005	0.0015	0.0013	0.0018	0.0012	0.0019	0.0027	0.0014
	κ	0.4301	0.8111	1.0000	1.0000	1.0000	1.0000	1.0000	1.0000	0.7104	1.0000	1.0000	1.0000	1.0000	1.0000
	ν	0.0462	0.0380	0.0500	0.0597	0.0695	0.0526	0.0304	0.0546	0.0000	0.0594	0.0498	0.0545	0.0649	0.0524
	ρ	-0.3608	0.0865	-0.0789	0.0598	-0.0021	-0.0575	-0.0664	-0.0556	0.9975	-0.0979	-0.0757	-0.1143	0.0984	-0.0114
Merton	μ	0.0016	0.0004	0.0013	0.0017	0.0010	0.0008	0.0010	0.0012	0.0005	0.0006	0.0006	0.0006	0.0005	0.0009
	σ	0.0366	0.0150	0.0290	0.0305	0.0331	0.0274	0.0154	0.0283	0.0314	0.0272	0.0257	0.0356	0.0378	0.0151
	μ_J	-0.0565	0.0009	-0.0284	-0.0068	-0.0032	-0.0075	-0.0080	-0.0108	0.0048	-0.0051	-0.0068	-0.0135	0.0043	-0.0013
	σ_J	0.0100	0.0175	0.0701	0.0595	0.0464	0.0478	0.0303	0.0570	0.0451	0.0416	0.0419	0.0578	0.0441	0.0241
	λ	0.3271	2.1353	0.1476	0.4020	0.7139	0.3949	0.4010	0.3644	0.3938	0.7407	0.4339	0.2313	0.6768	2.1147
Bates	μ	0.0016	0.0004	0.0013	0.0017	0.0010	0.0008	0.0010	0.0012	0.0005	0.0006	0.0006	0.0006	0.0005	0.0009
	v_0	0.0018	0.0007	0.0010	0.0013	0.0022	0.0012	0.0004	0.0013	0.0012	0.0015	0.0009	0.0017	0.0021	0.0004
	Θ	0.0018	0.0007	0.0010	0.0013	0.0022	0.0012	0.0004	0.0013	0.0012	0.0015	0.0009	0.0017	0.0021	0.0004
	κ	0.2575	0.2178	0.3718	0.5132	0.9264	0.9664	1.0000	1.0000	0.1430	1.0000	0.3928	0.3174	0.9980	0.8289
	ν	0.0303	0.0169	0.0276	0.0372	0.0639	0.0490	0.0259	0.0502	0.0185	0.0544	0.0267	0.0326	0.0302	0.0257
	ρ	-0.9760	0.5958	0.2138	0.5307	0.1402	0.1206	0.3662	0.2274	0.2257	0.1191	0.2967	-0.0577	0.6092	0.5377
	μ_J	0.0217	-0.0208	-0.0510	-0.0302	-0.0448	-0.0386	-0.0211	-0.0359	-0.0001	-0.0304	-0.0239	-0.0319	-0.0344	-0.0034
	σ_J	0.0100	0.0244	0.0472	0.0454	0.0676	0.0619	0.0180	0.0575	0.0585	0.0568	0.0349	0.1046	0.0596	0.0242
	λ	1.2574	0.2663	0.0866	0.2740	0.0774	0.0826	0.2309	0.1432	0.1948	0.1507	0.2540	0.0425	0.1825	1.6849

A4: In-sample APDF: Calibrated parameters (2)

Al: Aluminium, Cc: Cocoa, Cf: Coffee, Cn: Corn, Co: Copper, Go: Gold, Le: Lead, Ni: Nickel, Ol: Crude oil, Si: Silver, So: Soybeans, Su: Sugar, Wt: Wheat, Zi: Zinc. Calibration period: 02/08/1993 - 30/12/2013. Data frequency: Weekly.

		Ol	Al	Co	Le	Ni	Zi	Go	Si	Wt	Cn	So	Su	Cf	Cc
VG	μ	0.0299	-0.0076	-0.0009	-0.0061	-0.0022	-0.0001	0.0013	-0.0006	-0.0085	0.0018	0.0002	0.0061	-0.0170	-0.0001
	σ	0.0481	0.0295	0.0352	0.0441	0.0502	0.0386	0.0226	0.0407	0.0404	0.0438	0.0359	0.0430	0.0507	0.0390
	θ	-0.0290	0.0094	0.0044	0.0105	0.0038	0.0023	0.0003	0.0041	0.0087	0.0003	0.0019	-0.0054	0.0192	0.0012
	ν	0.2467	0.3028	0.3129	0.4787	0.3811	0.4275	0.4684	0.4803	0.2700	0.4411	0.3748	0.2365	0.2451	0.4733
NIG	μ	0.0359	-0.0075	0.0000	-0.0053	-0.0018	0.0004	0.0017	-0.0001	-0.0081	0.0021	0.0006	0.0059	-0.0163	0.0002
	α	45.9835	53.8220	40.1831	23.6594	24.6592	29.8166	42.8650	24.5062	39.4388	24.3330	34.5158	40.4122	34.6873	28.1036
	β	-15.8815	10.5939	2.6452	4.8301	1.2863	1.1253	-0.5028	2.0952	5.0376	-0.0831	1.0431	-2.7411	7.1252	0.4730
	δ	0.0963	0.0469	0.0521	0.0496	0.0659	0.0474	0.0249	0.0450	0.0662	0.0511	0.0473	0.0766	0.0894	0.0456
NIG-CIR	μ	0.0016	0.0004	0.0013	0.0017	0.0010	0.0008	0.0010	0.0012	0.0005	0.0006	0.0006	0.0006	0.0005	0.0009
	α	91.772	151.636	199.949	200.000	94.463	119.308	199.998	156.133	190.132	140.302	199.886	181.821	199.834	75.083
	β	-12.9433	4.5377	-3.4063	1.3090	-0.4712	-1.8732	-2.7510	-1.5719	3.7654	-2.5630	-2.8007	-4.9531	2.9558	-0.4453
	δ	0.2099	0.1330	0.2573	0.4193	0.4347	0.2552	0.1218	0.1579	0.1657	0.2614	0.2461	0.1888	0.4354	0.1128
	λ	0.7606	0.8235	2.1100	1.1682	1.9433	2.2305	2.6086	3.5489	2.7997	2.2607	2.4417	2.4902	1.1180	0.9663
	κ	0.0000	0.0000	2.1671	0.1121	3.0492	2.6911	2.3161	1.6841	2.2001	1.5160	2.0857	2.1645	0.3973	0.0000
	η	3.3483	3.9265	0.9985	0.0000	0.3664	0.5725	0.8373	2.4981	2.5348	1.1648	1.1537	2.3542	2.1759	0.6372

A5: Out-of-sample APDF: Calibrated parameters (1)

Al: Aluminium, Cc: Cocoa, Cf: Coffee, Cn: Corn, Co: Copper, Go: Gold, Le: Lead, Ni: Nickel, Ol: Crude oil, Si: Silver, So: Soybeans, Su: Sugar, Wt: Wheat, Zi: Zinc. Calibration period: 02/08/1993 - 27/12/2004. Data frequency: Weekly.

		Ol	Al	Co	Le	Ni	Zi	Go	Si	Wt	Cn	So	Su	Cf	Cc
GBM	μ	0.0055	-0.0002	0.0024	-0.0010	0.0017	0.0007	0.0003	0.0006	-0.0003	0.0000	-0.0001	0.0016	-0.0015	-0.0010
	σ	0.0491	0.0240	0.0284	0.0303	0.0400	0.0256	0.0155	0.0287	0.0322	0.0334	0.0290	0.0404	0.0566	0.0310
Heston	μ	0.0014	0.0008	0.0008	0.0016	0.0019	0.0005	0.0002	0.0004	0.0004	-0.0003	-0.0004	-0.0001	0.0006	0.0007
	v_0	0.0027	0.0007	0.0009	0.0011	0.0019	0.0008	0.0003	0.0010	0.0012	0.0014	0.0010	0.0020	0.0038	0.0012
	Θ	0.0027	0.0007	0.0009	0.0011	0.0019	0.0008	0.0003	0.0010	0.0012	0.0014	0.0010	0.0020	0.0038	0.0012
	κ	0.2974	0.4632	1.0000	1.0000	1.0000	1.0000	1.0000	1.0000	1.0000	1.0000	1.0000	1.0000	0.8001	1.0000
	ν	0.0400	0.0247	0.0298	0.0474	0.0624	0.0399	0.0243	0.0447	0.0407	0.0520	0.0454	0.0632	0.0784	0.0484
	ρ	-0.3809	0.1802	-0.1535	0.2409	-0.0072	0.0014	-0.0155	-0.0117	0.0449	-0.0169	-0.0331	-0.1530	0.1208	0.1012
Merton	μ	0.0014	0.0008	0.0008	0.0016	0.0019	0.0005	0.0002	0.0004	0.0004	-0.0003	-0.0004	-0.0001	0.0006	0.0007
	σ	0.0387	0.0231	0.0274	0.0157	0.0333	0.0080	0.0114	0.0165	0.0289	0.0201	0.0210	0.0385	0.0312	0.0141
	μ_J	-0.0544	-0.0098	-0.0647	0.0014	-0.0125	-0.0004	-0.0009	-0.0009	0.0002	0.0009	0.0010	-0.0724	0.0036	0.0004
	σ_J	0.0100	0.8601	0.0725	0.0226	0.0541	0.0163	0.0175	0.0237	0.0485	0.0297	0.0338	0.0100	0.0361	0.0240
	λ	0.3733	0.0525	0.0524	1.7990	0.3647	2.8529	0.6808	1.4448	0.2222	1.2510	0.6831	0.0504	2.1499	1.8882
Bates	μ	0.0014	0.0008	0.0008	0.0016	0.0019	0.0005	0.0002	0.0004	0.0004	-0.0003	-0.0004	-0.0001	0.0006	0.0007
	v_0	0.0026	0.0007	0.0008	0.0008	0.0007	0.0001	0.0002	0.0009	0.0008	0.0008	0.0009	0.0019	0.0030	0.0004
	Θ	0.0026	0.0007	0.0008	0.0008	0.0007	0.0001	0.0002	0.0009	0.0008	0.0008	0.0009	0.0019	0.0030	0.0004
	κ	0.2574	0.4401	0.0860	0.6730	0.3425	0.0347	0.2245	1.0000	0.0037	0.6022	1.0000	0.7904	0.2056	0.7811
	ν	0.0367	0.0241	0.0116	0.0324	0.0219	0.0020	0.0084	0.0422	0.0025	0.0313	0.0426	0.0553	0.0351	0.0247
	ρ	-0.3488	0.3158	0.1484	0.4284	0.8470	0.9997	0.4296	0.1156	1.0000	0.3635	0.2403	-0.1179	0.6354	-0.1913
	μ_J	-0.2000	-0.2000	-0.0555	-0.0025	-0.0061	0.0000	-0.0037	-0.0208	-0.0033	-0.0099	-0.0568	-0.0979	-0.0648	0.0034
	σ_J	0.4703	0.0549	0.0435	0.0306	0.0258	0.0161	0.0166	0.0633	0.0461	0.0334	0.0100	0.4336	0.0524	0.0264
	λ	0.0055	0.0076	0.0539	0.4613	1.8118	2.8929	0.5939	0.0900	0.2413	0.5867	0.0745	0.0087	0.1640	1.3032

A5: Out-of-sample APDF: Calibrated parameters (2)

Al: Aluminium, Cc: Cocoa, Cf: Coffee, Cn: Corn, Co: Copper, Go: Gold, Le: Lead, Ni: Nickel, Ol: Crude oil, Si: Silver, So: Soybeans, Su: Sugar, Wt: Wheat, Zi: Zinc. Calibration period: 02/08/1993 - 27/12/2004. Data frequency: Weekly.

		Ol	Al	Co	Le	Ni	Zi	Go	Si	Wt	Cn	So	Su	Cf	Cc
VG	μ	0.0363	-0.0115	0.0009	-0.0096	-0.0007	-0.0016	-0.0004	-0.0009	-0.0048	-0.0025	-0.0011	0.0080	-0.0201	-0.0021
	σ	0.0498	0.0251	0.0298	0.0338	0.0452	0.0294	0.0177	0.0330	0.0344	0.0387	0.0334	0.0443	0.0612	0.0370
	θ	-0.0350	0.0134	0.0017	0.0118	0.0032	0.0031	0.0008	0.0022	0.0052	0.0035	0.0014	-0.0081	0.0233	0.0017
	ν	0.1778	0.2380	0.1504	0.4240	0.3934	0.4514	0.4140	0.4457	0.2069	0.4706	0.4312	0.3102	0.3136	0.5514
NIG	μ	0.0475	-0.0122	0.0016	-0.0103	0.0000	-0.0017	0.0000	-0.0010	-0.0044	-0.0022	-0.0008	0.0083	-0.0203	-0.0024
	α	57.2743	78.9506	77.8373	37.7727	27.8747	42.1197	62.5417	32.2491	53.7035	26.5977	31.3370	34.1879	25.9510	24.0662
	β	-19.7443	22.7550	0.9113	11.2882	1.1159	3.8530	1.1330	2.0681	4.0839	2.0179	0.8702	-4.3370	6.3247	1.6120
	δ	0.1266	0.0475	0.0699	0.0428	0.0597	0.0371	0.0215	0.0385	0.0652	0.0437	0.0388	0.0685	0.0960	0.0373
NIG-CIR	μ	0.0014	0.0008	0.0008	0.0016	0.0019	0.0005	0.0002	0.0004	0.0004	-0.0003	-0.0004	-0.0001	0.0006	0.0007
	α	111.322	199.946	91.289	200.000	74.563	104.304	63.444	109.543	199.997	199.986	200.000	74.619	67.497	67.178
	β	-15.2681	12.5361	-2.5943	7.8808	-0.2985	0.0193	-0.5519	-0.8476	1.8085	-0.7430	-1.3066	-5.4945	2.7908	1.7719
	δ	0.2711	0.1285	0.1143	0.2300	0.1506	0.0892	0.0284	0.1393	0.1113	0.3035	0.2388	0.4158	0.2553	0.0500
	λ	0.6838	0.7320	0.0000	1.0636	0.8937	0.9567	0.0000	2.6020	2.9419	1.7077	2.4696	1.6710	0.8170	3.0680
	κ	0.0000	0.0000	2.5965	0.0000	0.0000	0.0000	0.5903	2.7609	2.8576	0.7635	1.9234	4.9565	0.0000	1.6467
	η	0.0428	4.8396	0.5452	0.3476	0.0268	0.4657	0.0386	0.8431	2.7391	1.0867	0.9945	0.1920	0.3607	2.7577

A6: Capital investment project: Valuation parameters

The table reports input parameter values for the stylised capital investment project used in the comparison of stochastic processes. The calibrated parameters for each process and resource can be found in appendix A4. Since calibrated parameters for the commodity price are in weekly units, the annual inputs shown below are converted to weeks where necessary. A simplified counting convention is used (50 weeks/year).

Project inputs:	
Project start:	02/01/2014
Total time horizon (T):	10 years
Maximum operating time:	5 years
Decision time horizon:	5 years
Aluminium production quantity (qr):	300 tons/year
Initial aluminium price (S0):	\$1776.8/ton
Variable production cost (c)	\$1700/ton
Fixed costs (K):	\$65,000/year
Tax rate (τ):	30%
Risk-free interest rate (r):	2%
Net convenience yield of aluminium (q):	0%
Salvage value (η):	\$20,000
Discretisation steps per time path	100
Number of paths	150,000

Appendix B

B1: Expected value and variance for GBM and the Vasicek model:

This part of the appendix shows how process mean and variance are calculated to produce fig. 3. The corresponding process discretisation and MLE implementation also used in this analysis are shown in the subsequent paragraph.
Considering first the case of GBM, Brigo et al. (2007) show that expected value $E[S(t)|S(0)]$ and variance $V[S(t)|S(0)]$ are given by

$$E[S(t)] = S(0)\exp\left(\mu t + \frac{\sigma^2 t}{2}\right)$$
$$V[S(t)] = S(0)^2 \exp(2\mu t)\left(\exp\left(\sigma^2 t\right) - 1\right).$$

In the case of the Vasicek model or Ornstein-Uhlenbeck process, expected value and variance are, for instance, reported by Brigo et al. (2007) and are given by

$$E[S(t)] = \mu + (S(0) - \mu)\exp(-\lambda t)$$
$$V[S(t)] = \frac{\sigma^2}{2\lambda}(1 - \exp(-2\lambda t)),$$

where μ denotes the long-run mean level of the process and λ the mean reversion speed.

B2: Maximum likelihood calibration:

The MLE method was used to calibrate parameters in the backtest presented in fig. 3 and the discussion on the quality of results obtained from the APDF algorithm in section 4.2.

GBM: In the case of GBM, the log-returns are a series of independent and identically distributed random variables, each with density $f_\theta(r) = f(f;\mu;\sigma)$ (Brigo et al., 2007). The return density is known to be normal and given by

$$f(\theta) = \mathcal{N}\left(\left(\mu - \frac{1}{2}\sigma^2\right)\Delta t, \sigma^2 \Delta t\right).$$

The MLE estimate of $\hat{\theta}$ i.e. the set of parameters is obtained by numerically maximising

$$\ln\mathcal{L}(\theta) = \sum_{t=1}^{T} \log f_\theta(r_t),$$

where T denotes the total number of return observations in the sample. The implementation is based on Brigo et al. (2007) and available, as all other calculations, in the Matlab package provided complementary to this thesis.

Vasicek: The Vasicek model is calibrated in levels not returns. The log-likelihood function for a set of (commodity) prices is given by

$$\begin{aligned}
\mathcal{L}(\mu,\lambda,\sigma) &= \sum_{t=1}^{T} \ln f(S(t)S(t-1);\mu;\lambda;\sigma) \\
&= -\frac{n}{2}\ln(2\pi) - T\ln(\sigma) \\
&\quad - \frac{1}{2\sigma^2}\sum_{t=1}^{T}\left[S(t) - S(t-1)\exp(-\lambda\Delta t) - \mu(1-\exp(-\lambda\Delta t))\right]^2.
\end{aligned}$$

Besides the possibility of numerical maximisation, explicit maximum likelihood equations can be derived.[56] Please note also that I verify the equivalence of parameter estimates under MLE and OLS regression calibration.

[56]For further reference see http://www.sitmo.com/article/calibrating-the-ornstein-uhlenbeck-model/.

Merton: The log-likelihood function for the set of historical returns r is given by

$$\begin{aligned} \ln \mathcal{L}(\theta) &= \sum_{t=1}^{T} \ln \left(r_t; \mu; \sigma; \mu_J; \sigma_J \right) \\ &= \sum_{j=0}^{+\infty} \mathrm{P}\left(T_t = j \right) f_{\mathcal{N}} = \left(r_t; \left(\mu - \frac{\sigma^2}{2} \right) dt + j\mu_J, \sigma^2 \Delta t + j\sigma_J^2 \right), \end{aligned}$$

which is an infinite mixture of Gaussian random variables, weighted by a Poisson probability $\mathrm{P}(T_t = j) = f_P(j; \lambda \Delta t)$ (Brigo et al., 2007).

Variance Gamma: In the estimation of the VG process parameters, I follow Brigo et al. (2007) and use the Matlab function *mle* to calculate the MLE estimates from the model probability density as given by (4.1.18). The numerical optimisation is initialised as follows:

$$\begin{aligned} \hat{\sigma} &= \sqrt{\frac{\sigma}{\Delta t}} \\ \hat{\nu} &= K1 \Delta t \\ \hat{\theta} &= \frac{S1 \hat{\sigma} \sqrt{\Delta t}}{3\nu} \\ \hat{\mu} &= \frac{\mu}{dt} - \hat{\theta}, \end{aligned}$$

where *K1* and *S1* are the standard measures for excess kurtosis and skewness outlined in section 3.2.1.

B3: Characteristic function and Fourier transforms

According to Schoutens (2003), the characteristic function ϕ of a distribution X, is the Fourier-Steltjes transform of the distribution function $F(x) = P(X \leq x)$:

$$\phi_x(u) = E\left[exp(iuX) \right] = \int_{-\infty}^{infty} \exp(iux)\, dF(x).$$

The characteristic function always exists and, in our context, characterises the return distribution of a stochastic process uniquely. In order to calculate the probability density on a discrete grid from the continuous characteristic function, the fast Fourier transform algorithm (*fft* in Matlab) is used. From an appropriate grid of N points, the characteristic function values x are transformed to the probability density X according to

$$X(k) = \sum_{j=1}^{N} x(j)\, \omega_N^{(j-1)(k-1)},$$

where

$$\omega_N = \exp\left(\frac{-2\pi i}{N}\right)$$

and i refers to the imaginary unit in complex numbers. The calculation of probability density on a discrete grid of N returns, requires an appropriate transformation of the return grid prior to computing corresponding characteristic function values and Fourier transform. The implementation of this procedure is available in the complementary Matlab file *fft_pdf*.

B4: Quadratic exponential scheme for Heston and Bates process

The discretisation used in this paper directly follows Kienitz and Wetterau (2012, p. 297) and involves the following algorithm:

1. Compute

$$m = \Theta + (V(t) - \Theta)\exp(-\kappa\Delta)$$

$$s^2 = \frac{V(t)\,\nu^2 e^{-\kappa\delta}}{\kappa}\left(1 - e^{-\kappa\Delta}\right) + \frac{\Theta\nu^2}{2\kappa}\left(1 - e^{-\kappa\Delta}\right)^2$$

2. For comparison calculate ψ

$$\psi = \frac{s^2}{m^2} = \frac{\frac{V(t)\nu^2 \exp(-\kappa\Delta)}{\kappa} \frac{\left(1-\exp(-\kappa\Delta)\Theta\nu^2\right)}{2\kappa} \left(1-\exp\left(-\kappa\Delta\right)\right)^2}{\left(\Theta + \left(V\left(t\right)-\Theta\right)\exp\left(-\kappa\Delta\right)\right)^2}$$

3. Generate $u \sim \mathcal{U}(0,1)$
4. Compute $V(t+\Delta)$ by switching rule

if $\psi \leq \psi_c$ **then**

Use a non-central χ^2 distribution for approximation and moment matching.

A: $b^2 = 2\psi^{-}1 - 1 + \sqrt{2/\psi^{-}1}\sqrt{s\psi^{-}1-1} \geq 0$ and $a = \frac{m}{1+b^2}$

B: Let z_1 denote a variate of $Z_1 \sim \mathcal{N}(0,1)$

C: Set $V(t+\Delta) = a\left(b+z_1\right)^2$

if $\psi > \psi_c$ **then**

Use an exponential distribution to approximate the true distribution. To generate variates from the exponential distribution apply the following rule:

A: Set $\left(p = \frac{\psi-1}{\psi+1}\right)$

B: Set $\beta = \frac{1-p}{m} = \frac{2}{m(\psi+1)}$

C: Set $V(t+\Delta) = \psi^{-}1\left(u;p,\beta\right)$ with

$$\psi^{-1}(u) = \psi^{-1}(u;p,\beta) = \begin{cases} 0 & \text{if } 0 \leq u \leq p \\ \beta^{-1}\log\left(\frac{1-p}{1-u}\right) & \text{if } p < u \leq 1 \end{cases}$$

5. Denoting by z_2 a realisation of $Z \sim \mathcal{N}(0,1)$, set

$$X(t+\Delta) = X(t) + K_0 + K_1 V(t) + K_2 V(t+\Delta) + \sqrt{K_3 V(t) + K_4 V(t+\Delta)}z_2.$$

For a grid with equidistant time steps, as used in this paper, $K_0, \ldots, K_4$ are constants and can be calculated according to:

$$K_0 = -\frac{\rho\kappa\Theta}{\nu}\Delta$$

$$K_1 = \gamma_1\Delta\left(\frac{\kappa\rho}{\nu} - \frac{1}{2}\right) - \frac{\rho}{\nu}$$

$$K_2 = \gamma_2\Delta\left(\frac{\kappa\rho}{\nu} - \frac{1}{2}\right) + \frac{\rho}{\nu}$$

$$K_3 = \gamma_1\Delta\left(1 - \rho^2\right)$$

$$K_4 = \gamma_2\Delta\left(1 - \rho^2\right).$$

The martingale correction for risk-neutral simulation in Monte Carlo-based valuation using the LSM algorithm, can be accomplished by replacing K_0 with

$$K_0^* = -\log(M) - (K_1 + 0.5K_3)V_n,$$

where the constant M can be computed explicitly when $\psi \leq \psi_c$ according to

$$M = \frac{\exp\left(\frac{Ab^2a}{1-2Aa}\right)}{\sqrt{1-2Aa}}, \quad A < \frac{1}{2a}.$$

When $\psi > \psi_c$ M is given by

$$M = p + \frac{\beta(1-p)}{\beta - A}, \quad A < \beta,$$

where

$$A = K_2 + 0.5K_4 = \frac{\rho}{\omega}(1 + \kappa\gamma_2\Delta) - 0.5\gamma_2\Delta\rho^2.$$

For further reference on the QE scheme, please refer to Andersen (2008) or Kienitz and Wetterau (2012) and for the Matlab implementation consider *path_heston* for the discretisation under the physical probability measure $\mathbb{P}$ and *path_heston_m* for the risk-neutral counterpart.

The corresponding implementation of the scheme adjusted for jumps as it is used for the Bates model simulation is provided in Matlab file *path_bates*.

B5: Basis functions and confidence intervals in LSM

Basis functions: The weighted Laguerre polynomials used in this paper were suggested by Longstaff and Schwartz (2001) and are given by

$$
\begin{aligned}
L_0(X) &= \exp\left(\frac{-X}{2}\right) \\
L_1(X) &= \exp\left(\frac{-X}{2}\right)(1-X) \\
L_2(X) &= \exp\left(\frac{-X}{2}\right)\left(1-2X+\frac{X^2}{2}\right) \\
L_n(X) &= \exp\left(\frac{-X}{2}\right)\left(\frac{e^X}{n!}\frac{d^n}{dX^n}\right)\left(X^n e^{-X}\right).
\end{aligned}
$$

The interested reader is also referred to Abramowitz and Stegun (1964) for a comprehensive overview of alternative orthogonal polynomials not considered in this thesis.

LSM confidence interval: These are computed according to Glasserman (2003) and Battauz and Ortu (2009). In particular, the radius of the confidence interval can be calculated as

$$\frac{\hat{\sigma}_n}{\sqrt{n}} z_{\frac{\delta}{2}},$$

where $\hat{\sigma}$ is the sample standard deviation of Monte Carlo estimates across paths, n is the number of simulated Monte Carlo paths, and δ is the confidence level (e.g. 95%). Note that the quantity $\hat{\sigma}_n/\sqrt{n}$ is often referred to as the standard error of estimates (Glasserman, 2003). More specifically, the volatility of estimates is given by

$$\hat{\sigma}_n = \sqrt{\frac{1}{n-1} \sum_{i=1}^{n} (V_i - \hat{\alpha}_n)^2},$$

where V_i is the Monte Carlo estimate of project value for commodity price path i in time zero and $\hat{\alpha}$ is the average value across paths i.e. the Monte Carlo estimate of project value. The upper and lower bound for valuation estimates can be computed by simply adding or subtracting the radius of the confidence interval to or from $\hat{\alpha}$.

References

Abramowitz, M., & Stegun, I. A. (1964). *Handbook of mathematical functions*. United States Department of Commerce.

Ait-Sahalia, Y., & Jacod, J. (2012). Analyzing the spectrum of asset returns: Jump and volatility components in high frequency data. *Journal of Economic Literature*, *50*(4), 1007 - 1050.

Akaike, H. (1973). Maximum likelihood identification of Gaussian auto-regressive moving-average models. *Biometrika*, *60*, 255-266.

Amihud, Y. (2002). Illiquidity and stock returns: Cross-section and time-series effects. *Journal of Financial Markets*, *5*(1), 31-56.

Andersen, L. (2008). Simple and efficient simulation of the Heston stochastic volatility model. *Journal of Computational Finance*, *11*, 11-42.

Anderson, T. W., & Darling, D. A. (1952). Asymptotic theory of certain "goodness of fit" criteria based on stochastic processes. *The Annals of Mathematical Statistics*, *23*(2), 193-212.

Bachelier, L. (1900). Theorie de la speculation. *Annales Scientifiques de l'Ecole Normale Superieure*, *3*(17), 21-86.

Bai, X., Russell, J. R., & Tiao, G. C. (2003). Kurtosis of GARCH and stochastic volatility models with non-normal innovations. *Journal of Econometrics*, *114*(2), 349 - 360.

Bakshi, G., Cao, C., & Zhiwu, C. (1997). Empirical performance of alternative option pricing models. *Journal of Finance*, *52*(5), 2003 - 2049.

Bates, D. (1996). Jumps and stochastic volatility: Exchange rate processes implicit in Deutsche Mark options. *Review of Financial Studies*, *9*, 69-107.

Battauz, A., & Ortu, F. (2009). *Arbitrage theory in discrete and continuous time*. EGEA lecture notes.

Bessembinder, H., Coughenour, J. F., Seguin, P. J., & Smoller, M. M. (1995). Mean reversion in equilibrium asset prices: Evidence from the futures term structure. *Journal of Finance, 50*(1), 361 - 375.

Bhappu, R. R., & Guzman, J. (1995). Mineral investment decision making: A study of mining company practices. *Engineering and Mining Journal, 70*, 36-38.

Björk, T. (2009). *Arbitrage theory in continuous time.* Oxford University Press.

Black, F., & Scholes, M. S. (1973). The pricing of options and corporate liabilities. *Journal of Political Economy, 81*, 637 - 654.

Bollerslev, T. (1986). Generalized autoregressive conditional heteroskedasticity. *Journal of Econometrics, 31*(3), 307 - 327.

Box, G. E. P., & Jenkins, G. (1994). *Time series analysis: Forecast and control.* Prentice Hall.

Boyarchenko, S. I., & Levendorskii, S. (2002). *Non-Gaussian Merton-Black-Scholes theory.* World Scientific.

Brealey, R. A., Allen, F., & Myers, S. C. (2011). *Principles of corporate finance.* McGraw-Hill.

Brennan, M. J. (1991). The price of convenience and the valuation of commodity contingent claims. In *Stochastic models and option values: Applications to resources, environment and investment problems* (p. 33 - 71). UCLA: Contributions to Economic Analysis, no. 200.

Brennan, M. J., & Schwartz, E. S. (1985). Evaluating natural resource investments. *Journal of Business, 58*, 135-157.

Brigo, D., Dalessandro, A., Neugebauer, M., & Triki, F. (2007). A stochastic processes toolkit for risk management. Retrieved from `http://ssrn.com/abstract=1109160`

Broadie, M., & Kaya, z. (2006). Exact simulation of stochastic volatility and other affine jump diffusion processes. *Operations Research, 54*(2), 217 - 231.

Brooks, C., & Prokopczuk, M. (2013). The dynamics of commodity prices. *Quantitative Finance, 13*(4), 527-542.

Carr, P., Geman, H., Madan, D., & Yor, M. (2003). Stochastic volatility for Lévy processes. *Mathematical Finance, 13*(3), 345-382.

Casassus, J., & Collin-Dufresne, P. (2005). Stochastic convenience yield implied from commodity futures and interest rates. *Journal of Finance, 60*, 2283-2331.

Cecchetti, S. G., & Pok-sang, L. (1994). Variance-ratio tests: Small-sample properties with an application to international output data. *Journal of Business & Economic Statistics, 12*(2), 177 - 186.

Cochrane, J. H. (1988). How big is the random walk in GNP? *Journal of Political Economy, 96*(5), 893-920.

Cont, R. (2001). Empirical properties of asset returns: Stylized facts and statistical issues. *Quantitative Finance, 1*, 223-236.

Cont, R., & Tankov, P. (2004). *Financial modelling with jump processes*. Chapman & Hall.

Copeland, T. E., & Antikarov, V. (2003). *Real options: A practitioner's guide.* Cengage Learning.

Cox, J. C., Ingersoll, J., Jonathan E., & Ross, S. A. (1985). A theory of the term structure of interest rates. *Econometrica, 53*(2), 385-408.

Cox, J. C., Ross, & Rubinstein, M. (1979). Option pricing: A simplified approach. *Journal of Financial Economics, 7*, 229-263.

Cryer, J. D., & Chan, K.-S. (2008). *Time series analysis with applications in R.* Springer.

De Laurentis, G., Maino, R., & Molteni, L. (2010). *Developing, validating and using internal ratings*. John Wiley & Sons.

Dickey, D. A., & Fuller, W. A. (1979). Distribution of the estimators for autoregressive time series with a unit root. *Journal of the American Statistical Association, 74*, 427-431.

Dickey, D. A., & Fuller, W. A. (1981). Likelihood ratio statistics for autoregressive time series with a unit root. *Econometrica, 49*, 1057-1072.

Dixit, A. K., & Pindyck, R. S. (1994). *Investment under uncertainty.* Princeton

University Press.

Elliot, L. (2011). Global financial crisis: Five key stages 2007-2011. *The Guardian*. Retrieved from http://www.theguardian.com/business/2011/aug/07/global-financial-crisis-key-stages

Engle, R. F. (1982). Autoregressive conditional heteroscedasticity with estimates of the variance of United Kingdom inflation. *Econometrica*, *50*(4), 987-1007.

Erb, C. B., & Harvey, C. R. (2005). *The tactical and strategic value of commodity futures* (Working Paper No. 11222). National Bureau of Economic Research.

Esty, B. C. (2004). Why study large projects? An introduction to research on project finance. *European Financial Management*, *10*, 213-224.

Fama, E. F. (1965). Random walks in stock market prices. *Journal of Business*, *38*, 34-105.

Fama, E. F., & French, K. R. (1987). Commodity future prices: Some evidence on forecast power, premiums, and the theory of storage. *Journal of Business*, *60*, 55-73.

Franke, J., Härdle, W. K., & Hafner, C. M. (2011). *Statistics of financial markets*. Springer.

Gamba, A. (2003). *Real options: A monte carlo approach.*

Gibson, R., & Schwartz, E. S. (1990). Stochastic convenience yield and the pricing of oil contingent claims. *Journal of Finance*, *45*, 959-976.

Glasserman, P. (2003). *Monte carlo methods in financial engineering*. Springer.

Gorton, G., & Rouwenhorst, K. G. (2006). Facts and fantasies about commodity futures. *Financial Analysts Journal*, *62*(2), 47 - 68.

Goyenko, R. Y., Holden, C. W., & Trzcinka, C. A. (2009). Do liquidity measures measure liquidity? *Journal of Financial Economics*, *92*(2), 153-181.

Gujarati, D. N. (2003). *Basic econometrics.* McGraw-Hill.

Heston, S. L. (1993). A closed-form solution for options with stochastic volatility with applications to bond and currency options. *Review of Financial Studies*, *6*(2), 327 - 343.

Hull, J. (2009). *Options, futures, and other derivatives.* Pearson/Prentice Hall.

Jarque, C. M., & Bera, A. K. (1987). A test for normality of observations and regression residuals. *International Statistical Review*, *55*(2), 163-172.

Kat, H. M., & Oomen, R. C. A. (2007). What every investor should know about commodities part I: Univariate return analysis. *Journal of Investment Management*, *5*(1), 4 - 28.

Kienitz, J., & Wetterau, D. (2012). *Financial modelling: Theory, implementation and practice*. Wiley.

Koller, T., Wessels, D., & Goedhart, M. (2010). *Valuation: Measuring and managing the value of companies.* Wiley.

Laughton, D. G., & Jacoby, H. D. (1993). Reversion, timing options, and long-term decision-making. *Financial Management*, *22*(3), 225 - 240.

Lesmond, D. A., Ogden, J. P., & Trzcinka, C. A. (1999). A new estimate of transaction costs. *Review of Financial Studies*, *12*(5), 1113 - 1141.

Ljung, G. M., & Box, G. E. P. (1978). On a measure of lack of fit in time series models. *Biometrika*, *65*(2), 297.

Lo, A. W., & Wang, J. (1995). Implementing option pricing models when asset returns are predictable. *Journal of Finance*, *50*, 87-129.

Longstaff, F. A., & Schwartz, E. S. (2001). Valuing American options by simulation: A simple least-squares approach. *Review of Financial Studies*, *14*.

Lund, D. (1992). *With timing options and heterogeneous costs, the lognormal diffusion is hardly an equilibrium price process for exhaustible resources* (Memorandum No. 03/1992). Oslo University, Department of Economics.

Madan, D. B., & Seneta, E. (1990). The variance gamma (V.G.) model for share market returns. *The Journal of Business*, *63*(4), 511-524.

Manoliu, M., & Tompaidis, S. (2002). Energy futures prices: Term structure models with Kalman filter estimation. *Applied Mathematical Finance*, *9*(1), 21 - 43.

Mantegna, R. N., & Stanley, H. E. (2000). *An introduction to econophysics:*

Correlations and complexity in finance. Cambridge University Press.

Marshall, B. R., Nguyen, N. H., & Visaltanachoti, N. (2012). Commodity liquidity measurement and transaction costs. *Review of Financial Studies*, *25*(2), 599 - 638.

Merton, R. C. (1976). Option pricing when underlying stock returns are discontinuous. *Journal of Financial Economics*, *3*, 125 - 144.

Metcalf, G. E., & Hassett, K. A. (1995). Investment under alternative return assumptions comparing random walks and mean reversion. *Journal of Economic Dynamics and Control*, *19*, 1471-1488.

Nissanke, M. (2012). Commodity market linkages in the global financial crisis: Excess volatility and development impacts. *Journal of Development Studies*, *48*(6), 732 - 750.

Ozorio, L., Bastian-Pinto, C., & Brandao, L. (2011). *The choice of stochastic process in real option valuation.* Retrieved from `http://realoptions.org/openconf2012/data/papers/49.pdf`

Parzen, E. (1962). On estimation of a probability density function and mode. *The Annals of Mathematical Statistics*, *33*(3), 1065-1076.

Pindyck, R. S. (1999). The long-run evolution of energy prices. *Energy Journal*, *20*, 1.

Razali, N. M. (2011). Power comparison of Shapiro-Wilk, Kolmogorov-Smirnov, Lilliefors and Anderson-Darling tests. *Journal of Statistical Modeling and Analytics*, *2*(1), 21-33.

Richter, M., & Sörensen, C. (2003). Stochastic volatility and seasonality in commodity futures and options: The case of soybeans (working paper). *Frederiksberg, Denmark: Copenhagen Business School.*

Roberts, K., & Weitzman, M. (1981). Funding criteria for research, development, and exploration projects. *Econometrica*, *49*(5), 1261 - 1288.

Roberts, M., & Schlenker, W. (2013). Identifying supply and demand elasticities of agricultural commodities: Implications for the US ethanol mandate. *American*

Economic Review, *103*(6), 2265 - 2295.

Ross, S. A. (1997). Hedging long run commitments: Exercises in incomplete market pricing. *Economic Notes*, *26*(2), 385 - 419.

Samuelson, P. A. (1964). Proof that properly anticipated prices fluctuate randomly. *Industrial Management Review*, *6*(1), 41 - 49.

Schoutens, W. (2003). *Lévy processes in finance*. John Wiley & Sons.

Schuh, C., Strohmer, M., & Zetterqvist, S. (2011). *Raw material strategy - volatility is here to stay.* Retrieved from `http://www.atkearney.de/metals-mining/ideas-insights/article/-/asset_publisher/LCcgOeS4t85g/content/raw-material-strategy-volatility-is-here-to-stay`

Schulmerich, M. (2010). *Real options valuation: The importance of interest rate modelling in theory and practice*. Springer.

Schwartz, E. S. (1997). The stochastic behavior of commodity prices: Implications for valuation and hedging. *Journal of Finance*, *52*, 923-973.

Schwartz, E. S. (2004). Patents and R&D as real options. *Economic Notes*, *33*(1), 23 - 54.

Schwartz, E. S., & Miltersen, K. R. (1998). Pricing of options on commodity futures with stochastic term structures of convenience yields and interest rates. *Journal of Financial and Quantitative Analysis*, *33*, 33-59.

Schwartz, E. S., & Smith, J. (2000). Short-term variations and long-term dynamics in commodity prices. *Management Science*, *46*, 893-911.

Schwert, G. W. (1989). Tests for unit roots: A Monte Carlo investigation. *Journal of Business & Economic Statistics*, *7*, 147-159.

Seneta, E. (2004). Fitting the variance-gamma model to financial data. *Journal of Applied Probability*, *41*, 177-187.

Sick, G., & Gamba, A. (2010). Some important issues involving real options: An overview. *Multinational Finance Journal*, *14*, 157-207.

Siegel, D., Smith, J., & Paddock, J. (1987). Valuing offshore oil properties with option pricing models. *Midland Corporate Finance Journal*, *5*, 22-30.

Silverman, B. W. (1986). *Density estimation for statistics and data analysis.* Chapman & Hall.

Stephens, M. A. (1974). EDF statistics for goodness of fit and some comparisons. *Journal of the American Statistical Association*, *69*(347), 730-737.

Storn, R., & Price, K. (1995). *Differential evolution - a simple and efficient adaptive scheme for global optimization over continuous spaces.* Retrieved from `http://www1.icsi.berkeley.edu/ftp/pub/techreports/1995/tr-95-012.pdf`

Tang, K. (2012). Time-varying long-run mean of commodity prices and the modeling of futures term structures. *Quantitative Finance*, *12*(5), 781 - 790.

Trigeorgis, L. (1996). *Real options: Managerial flexibility and strategy in resource allocation.* MIT Press.

Tsekrekos, A. E., Shackleton, M. B., & Wojakowski, R. (2012). Evaluating natural resource investments under different model dynamics: Managerial insights. *European Financial Management*, *18*, 543-575.

Vasicek, O. (1977). An equilibrium characterization of the term structure. *Journal of Financial Economics*, *5*, 177-188.

Yungchih Wang, G. (2011). Examining the uncertainty-investment relationship under various stochastic processes. *Banking and Finance Review*, *3*, 1-21.

MIX
Papier aus verantwortungsvollen Quellen
Paper from responsible sources
FSC® C105338

If you have any concerns about our products,
you can contact us on
ProductSafety@springernature.com

In case Publisher is established outside the EU,
the EU authorized representative is:
Springer Nature Customer Service Center GmbH
Europaplatz 3, 69115 Heidelberg, Germany

Printed by Libri Plureos GmbH
in Hamburg, Germany